JESUS ON THE CROSS WHY?

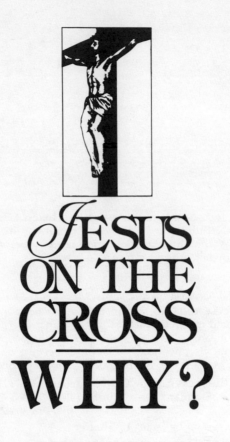

JESUS ON THE CROSS — WHY?

Philip A. St. Romain

AVE MARIA PRESS NOTRE DAME, INDIANA 46556

Library of Congress Catalog Card Number: 87-70903
International Standard Book Number: 0-87793-363-4
                                    0-87793-364-2(pbk.)
Cover photograph by James L. Shaffer
Cover and text design: Katherine A. Coleman
Printed and bound in the United States of America.

Philip A. St. Romain works as a writer, lecturer and counsellor
through his company, Personal Growth Services, 13586 Neil
Ave., Baton Rouge, LA 70810, (504) 766-7615.

Contents

	Foreword	9
	Prologue	15
One	Suffering Servant	25
Two	Lamb of God	35
Three	Prince of Peace	47
Four	Immanuel	61
Five	Savior of the World	77
Six	The Way of the Cross	91
	Appendix One: Questions for Reflection and Discussion	105
	Appendix Two: Suggested Reading	109

Acknowledgments

To list the many people who have helped me through the years to understand the meaning of the cross would be impossible. Deserving special mention, however, are my parents, who have taught me much about persevering in love through both good times and bad. My best friend, Herman Sensat, died of cancer in October, 1985. It was a long and painful struggle, but both he and his wife, Pat, taught me that people can remain human even in the face of death.

My wife, Lisa, has also inspired me many times with her courage during times of suffering. Anyone who undergoes pregnancy and labor in order to bring new life into the world is to be commended. Lisa has made this sacrifice three times thus far in our married life. Her selfless care for our children is also a testimony to the power of the cross.

I mention here, too, my grandparents, and their struggles with aging and death, and again my parents and their brothers and sisters, who sat with them through many very long days and nights in the hospital.

Other inspiring testimonies to the resiliency of the human spirit have been those alcoholics and drug addicts I have counseled through the years. Many of these people have been through hell on earth, but they nonetheless find the strength to forgive themselves and move along.

Through all these models of cross-bearing in my family and in my work, I have learned more about the paschal mystery than in all the books of theology I have read on this topic.

Theology books and discussions are important, however; without a map of some kind, we can get lost. Several significant theological dialogue partners who have influenced this book include Father John Edmonds, S.T., Sister Lydia Champagne and Father Robert Marcel. Father Edmonds has also read this manuscript and provided helpful suggestions concerning theology and development.

Foreword

One of my earliest recollections from parochial school days concerns the meaning of the crucifixion. It was nearing Holy Week, and Sister had been teaching us second-graders about Jesus' redemptive death. "He died for you," she told us, "so that you could live without sin and be happy with God forever." I was already feeling uneasy about the prospect of living with God forever, not quite sure that this was going to be as fun as Sister made it out to be. In addition, I was very confused about why Jesus had to die. I didn't see how he could have died for me, since he never knew me in the first place, and I hadn't done anything so wrong as to bring about his death. The whole thing left me feeling terribly guilty, like someone had done me a great favor and put me in great debt, but I hadn't asked for the favor in the first place.

Through my childhood and even later years, the theology of the crucifixion which I was taught featured such concepts as ransom, debt, expiation, atonement, sacrifice and satisfaction. The story goes—

and I know you've heard it—that in the beginning, Adam and Eve walked and talked with God. Then God gave them an obedience test, which they flunked, so God sent them out of the Garden of Eden and closed the gates of heaven. God wasn't happy about this situation, however, so he formed a people, the Jews, and prepared them for the coming of a messiah. We Christians believe Jesus is that messiah. As true God and true man, Jesus was the only one who could repay the debt of Adam and Eve. This he did by dying on the cross, becoming a ransom for us and the perfect sacrifice who bridged the gap between God and humanity.

As a young child, I found justice in this account, but also something cruel and disturbing. After all, it only seemed right that people should be punished when they did something wrong, and that this punishment should make things right again. But somehow it didn't seem right that an innocent person should be punished for the guilty, although there was certainly something admirable about that. I knew I would never volunteer to be punished for my sister's mistakes (in fact, I sometimes enjoyed watching her get her licks). It took a real hero to take somebody else's punishment, I guess. The only problem with this view was that my parents would never agree to such an arrangement. When my sister did wrong, punishing me would not help her at all. So how could God's punishing Jesus help Adam and Eve, who were dead at any rate? How could it help me, if it happened before I had done anything wrong? And what kind of God was this anyhow, wanting to punish someone—anyone, but most especially his own son—to get rid of his anger! My parents never punished me just to get rid of their anger. Was God as good as my parents?

I grew up in a church which cherished the cross as the symbol of what we were about, but I did not understand its meaning. In Lent I saw many people piously and tearfully meditating on the Way of the Cross. To me, the passion and death of Jesus seemed monstrously cruel and gruesome—nothing to get piously enthusiastic about. Not trusting my own judgment, however, I kept telling myself that one day I would understand. High school came, then college, and I kept waiting to understand. Then several friends converted to Fundamentalist communities, and they seemed to be very excited about the cross. They spoke or being "washed in the blood of the Lamb." Gross stuff! I went to hear their preachers, and there it was all over again: Jesus dying on the cross as a ransom for my sins. Ransom? I was not even clear about what it meant to be a hostage!

Yet God's grace is such that I was never completely able to shake free of my attraction to Jesus. What I'd learned about him in my religion classes and through my own reading revealed a man who deeply inspired me. Through his eyes, I also came to see a loving Father, whose rain falls on the good and the bad alike. After coming to an adult faith commitment in my early 20s, I began to follow Jesus as my Lord of love, and to experience his risen presence in many different ways. As for my understanding of the crucifixion, I just simply accepted the fact that it was inevitable that a good and prophetic man like Jesus be killed by political and religious authorities more interested in preserving the status quo. Theologies of satisfaction and substitutionary atonement were still repulsive to me, but these were the only explanations I encountered.

I recall a particularly disturbing incident during my early days of adult faith when I was watching a televised Mass. In his homily, the priest told a story about a father who worked the controls at a railroad drawbridge. One day the father's only son, a young boy, came to play. The father warned him about playing near the machinery below, then went about his business. After a while a boat approached, so he opened the drawbridge to let it through. He then received word that a train was coming very soon and that he should close the bridge so it could pass over the stream. At that moment he looked out of his window and saw his son (his only beloved son!) playing near the control machinery below. If he closed the bridge, he would crush his son; if he didn't close it, a train full of people would fall into the river and drown. You can guess how the story ends.

I was bewildered and infuriated! How could my beloved Jesus and his Father be mixed up in such a gruesome business? How could a Catholic priest tell such a story over television? To make matters worse, I heard the same story from the pulpit the very next week (apparently, it was making the rounds). It was then that I decided that theologies of substitionary atonement did not answer my deepest questions about the crucifixion, although I didn't have anything to take their place.

Happily, I have since been introduced to several excellent books that helped me to reconcile my belief in a loving God with the events of Holy Week. My own prayer, reflection and struggles to live the gospel have also taught me much about the cross. Unfortunately, old explanations still seem to persist among both laity and clergy. That is why I am writing this book.

Why did Jesus die on the cross?

There are many different levels of response to this question. A historian, for example, would interpret the question *why* in different terms than a psychologist or theologian. The historian would probably say that Jesus died on the cross because he was perceived by the Jewish authorities as threatening their already tenuous political relationship with Rome. A psychologist might say that the love of Jesus called people to change, and few people arouse more hatred in us than those who provoke us out of spiritual inertia. The theologian, on the other hand, is primarily interested in what God has accomplished through the crucifixion of Jesus of Nazareth. Our primary concern in this book shall be with theology. As we shall see, there are rich and wonderful approaches to understanding the crucifixion which better emphasize God's love than the traditional explanations of satisfaction and substitutionary atonement.

In reflecting upon the theology of the crucifixion, we shall begin with the early church. What did the crucifixion mean to the first Christians? Chapter 1 discusses the crucifixion as the fulfillment of the prophecies about the suffering servant of Yahweh, and Chapter 2 discusses the crucifixion as the fulfillment of traditions of sacrifice and covenant. These were the explanations which nourished the early church's theology of the crucifixion. Also in the early church we find the beginnings of a theology which recognizes the crucifixion as the means by which God broke the

13

power of sin rooted in the devil (Chapter 3), the flesh (Chapter 4), and the world (Chapter 5).

A second objective for the book is to discuss whether the understanding of the crucifixion reached by the early church and augmented through the ages still speaks to people of our age. How meaningful is it, for example, to speak of Jesus' death as a sacrifice to people who lack traditions of sacrifice in their culture? Chapters 2, 3, 4 and 5 include a section on catechetical implications which deal with these kinds of questions.

A third objective is to reflect on the meaning of the cross in our everyday lives. This is the main focus of Chapter 6. There we note the relationship between loving and laying down our lives for our friends. In this way, we come to better understand Jesus' words: "If anyone wishes to come after me, he must deny his very self, take up his cross, and follow in my steps" (Mk 8:34).

Like its companion, *Jesus Alive in Our Lives* (Ave Maria Press, 1985), which studied the meaning of the resurrection, this book will provide questions for reflection and discussion. I suggest that the reader spend some time with the questions in Appendix One, perhaps using a journal. It is also good to discuss a book of this kind with others to learn how they understand and experience the cross of Christ in their lives. Helping one another to carry our crosses is one of our most significant activities as church.

Philip St. Romain

Prologue

There once was a great council in heaven. Its purpose was to discuss the situation existing on earth, for it appeared that things were going badly. Angels were called in to give their reports to the Godhead. Some described the movements of the continents, others the various kinds of plants and animals. But of primary interest to all were recent developments among humans. Since the Shadow had invaded their hearts, it seemed to be spreading through them to disrupt the entire creation. The Godhead listened to all the reports in perfect silence, then encouraged and affirmed the angels before dismissing them.

"It sounds terrible!" said Logos Kyrios. "The darkness is truly upon them, and they seem powerless to break its hold."

"It *is* terrible!" agreed Spiritus. "Everything becomes twisted for them now. Where once humans felt at one with their world, now they feel apart from it. They consider it their enemy, to be overcome and manipulated to their own ends. Little do they realize that the earth is their mother, and that it is the Dark One's

15

desire that they eventually destroy the breasts that feed them."

"How I wish now we could help them to see their plight!" lamented Logos. "How I wish it were as in days of old: walking and talking with each other, delighting in creation. . . ."

"You may try as you wish to talk with them, but they get it all twisted," replied Spiritus. "The claws of the Dark One have scratched into their very souls, you see. Where once they loved life, now they fear death. And this fear is so powerful that it contaminates everything I have tried to tell them. This fear causes them to become controlling and manipulative, ever attempting to cheat death, or to prolong life. They grasp at their former glory, but it quickly degenerates into a lust for pleasure, or power, or material security. Left to themselves, the Dark One will plunder the planet, erasing all signs of the beauty and goodness we placed there."

"Then maybe we should vanquish the Dark One," offered Logos Kyrios. "Maybe it is time to send it away to a dark corner of the universe, where it may work no more destruction."

"That will not do," stated the First One, the creator of all that is. "For one thing, I promised Satan he could keep the spoils, and I cannot go back on my word. Secondly, vanquishing Satan will not now alter the grip of the darkness upon them. Already we see the disintegration that is taking place. This will continue even in Satan's absence, for it has come to be part of their traditions. Then there is the matter of the claw mark. Satan has gotten his claw into their spiritual realm, and there it will remain even if he is vanquished."

"So what is to be done?" queried Kyrios, exasperated. "Somehow it does not seem right to leave humans under the sway of the mightiest of the fallen."

"Do not forget that Satan has been denied permission to overwhelm them," retorted the Father. "Satan may tempt, but the freedom to choose is theirs. They have chosen to follow the Dark One, and so now they are paying the price."

"Yet every day it seems they grow *weaker* in freedom," objected Spiritus. "I am constantly appealing to them, but the world in which they live and the venom of the claw mark grow closer in likeness. So few of them respond!"

"They have forgotten who they are, then," concluded Logos.

"They have forgotten who they are," agreed Spiritus. "They have now become children of darkness."

After a period of sorrowful quiet, Logos ventured another suggestion. "Maybe we should make a grand showing of our splendor. If they could see us as we truly are, then they would find themselves. They are, after all, like unto our nature."

"That would not do either," countered the First One. "If we let them see us as we are, they would surely die, for they are mortals yet, and it is not for mortals to see us in this manner. But even if we could show ourselves thus, they would quickly forget. The very next generation would call the witnesses deluded and superstitious. Finally, the situation is such that already there are humans who have become filled with the darkness. If we revealed ourselves, they would turn from us and fly into Satan's stronghold. There they would be lost forever. While they live, however, there is yet hope that they will shake the darkness."

"But *how*?" exclaimed Logos in love's anguish. "It seems the only way is to remove their freedom. If they have no freedom, then they cannot fall prey to Satan."

"That is not an option," objected the First. "What has been created has been created. The humans were created to share freely in our love—a very great privilege extended to only a few groups in the universe. To remove their freedom would be to deny their humanity, and this simply will not do. Better by far to have only a few humans accept their heritage than to unmake them into simple animals who follow only instinct."

"Then *what* are we to do?" replied Logos Kyrios. "If, we have heard, the splendor of creation no longer reminds them of you, dear Father; and if Spiritus finds her efforts to inspire love frustrated by the mark of the Dark One, then it seems we can do nothing but watch as Satan plunders the planet. This prospect fills me with sadness!"

The First One smiled in deepest sympathy upon Kyrios while Spiritus filled his great heart with consolation. After a while, the Creator asked: "What do you think it would take to save the humans?"

"If only I knew!" lamented Logos. "I would do anything!"

"What do humans fear most?"

"Death! Unquestionably, death!" interjected Spiritus.

"Why do they fear death?" persisted the First One.

"Because of the claw of the Dark One," replied Spiritus again. She was very familiar with the insides of human nature.

At this, the First One started in on a new dream. "What if there were, even now, a human who could live the kind of life we intended them to live? Could this person not teach others the way to live?"

"There has not been such a person since the first ones fell," replied Spiritus. "And I am sure the race cannot now produce such a person. I have been trying for centuries to do just that, but the powers of darkness always seem to overwhelm them."

"What if this human were to be born without the mark of the claw?" returned the Creator.

Spiritus was ready for this one, too, having thought of it before an infinity of times. "Even if this were possible—and it would take an intervention on our part to exempt one of them from the mark—then we would be back to where we were at the beginning, when we first placed our own seal into their souls. Only things would be much worse now than before, for now the Dark Shadow contaminates human culture, where before it was but a tiny spark of static amidst the joyful harmony of all creation. So, even given a person free from the Shadow, the pervasive darkness would certainly conquer.

"Then just think of what Satan would do if we created such a new person—free from the claws of darkness. Satan would immediately note the existence of such a person, and would be quite suspicious of the whole thing. Surely a massive attack would be unleashed to kill, or disfigure, or corrupt this new person. For such a person to live as a normal human being—in loving fellowship with us and all of creation—would be an almost impossible task."

"What if this human being possessed wisdom and power greater than Satan's?" the First One replied.

19

"That would *truly* be a new person," agreed Spiritus. "But, as you know, in all the universe only a few archangels can rival Satan in spiritual power—and sometimes I'm not even sure about that. At any rate, archangels are archangels, and they would probably make very poor humans."

"Are you planning to create a new race of humans to live among the old, dear Father?" asked Logos, who had been listening hopefully to the First One's dreams.

"A new race could not save the old," objected Spiritus. "And don't forget that a new race would have to suffer a greater onslaught of darkness than the old. Then if they, too, with their greater spiritual powers, fell victims to Satan's spell of fear, they would become oppressors of the present race. Then where would we be?"

"Then *who* will save the humans from the kingdom of darkness?" asked the First One.

They were silent for a while, then the First One placed his dream in the heart of Kyrios. Kyrios gazed at the Majesty in awe as understanding came to him, while Spiritus spoke the words of their heart.

"What is needed is for another human—a member of their own race—to overcome the power of darkness. This may be done only if a human is capable of persisting in the life we intended them to live—in love and wisdom—while at the same time confronting the powers of darkness. Such a human would have to be free from the mark of the claw, and possess powers greater than Satan. Only such a human could meet the full onslaught of Satan while remaining faithful to his or her humanity. In order to completely break the reign of terror, this human would have to demonstrate conclusively the emptiness of Satan's reign of fear. This human would have to be mocked and scorned and tortured and, finally, killed, for these are the weapons by which the Dark One has enslaved them. If such a human were thus to enter the enemy's camp and emerge victorious, then humans would be able to see and believe that their destiny is with us. They might be able to hope in goodness again, and so experience me drawing them into our love. They might again find the strength to love one another, and they would be able to begin putting their world back together."

Logos Kyrios understood the invitation, but was weighing the implications. "I would have to become one of them, then," he finally admitted.

"It would be the best way to save many of them," agreed Spiritus.

"I would have to become a human being, and experience all the limitations that go with the race," Logos muttered, thinking aloud.

"It would truly require an emptying of your glory," Spiritus affirmed, marveling at the splendor of Logos and trying to imagine how it could be contained in human form.

"But I would be with you always," promised the First One.

"And I would join us with everyone and everything you come into contact with," consoled Spiritus.

"Yes, of course," Logos replied, acknowledging their reassurance. "But *I* would be the one to be tortured. . .and mocked. . .and scorned. . .and die as humans die," he stated now, counting the cost.

The Creator saw his torment and understood. "Yes, my Son," he consoled, "but it is the best way to rout the forces of the Dark One, is it not?"

"The best way," agreed Spiritus.

Logos thought this over a moment, then asked: "And after I have died a human death, what then?"

"A new race begins out of the old," promised the Creator. "You shall be the first-born in a new creation, which shall spring forth amidst the old and eventually transform the old. After your death will come the resurrection of humanity, for henceforth you shall always be true God and true man. Where there are humans, there shall we be. Those who are baptized in your way shall be rid of the mark of the claw, and they, too, shall be called upon to vanquish the darkness with the light of our love. They shall follow the path you have cleared through the heart of the Dark One's camp, but they will not be afraid. Death for them shall be as death for you: a mere transition into a state of glory greater than that which humans lost when Satan set his claw into their hearts."

"Then let me go now, Father, before the darkness is complete," Logos Kyrios volunteered, accepting his mission.

"Not so fast, my Son," the First One advised. "All is not lost even now. As long as creation stands and Spiritus whispers into the hearts of people, the darkness shall not completely conquer. If you were to go to them now, they would not accept you, nor would they understand your mission. We must prepare them for your coming, and that will take a few centuries. Even then, you will not be recognized by many—save the minions of Satan. *They* will know you from the moment you are born, and their treachery shall not cease until they have killed you."

Logos thought this over for a while, then asked

one final question. "Since my spiritual power is greater than Satan's, how could I break the spell of darkness as a *human being*? Would it not be necessary for me to renounce my power in order to do so?"

The First One smiled in understanding, then spoke gently. "As both human and divine, your power shall exceed that of Satan and his entire army. Evil, suffering and death shall obey your commands. But Satan knows very well the affairs of humans, and he will do everything possible to strike at your human weakness and lead you to misuse your power. For a while you must put him off, that you may establish your teaching and show them signs of my favor. Having done so, you must then enter into the camp of the enemy to break its hold. While in his camp, you will be tempted to use your power to save yourself, but you must not do so or he will retreat from you. No, when your final hour comes, you must renounce your power completely, trusting only in the goodness you have known here. Then will come the hour of darkness and the trial of all humanity!

"You will be treated as the most vile of humans, and you will experience great pain and anguish such as few have ever known. Although we shall never desert you, it will seem that way to you. It is then, during the hour of your torment and seeming abandonment, that you shall be put to the test in behalf of the human race. You shall be permitted to choose, as the first ones were permitted, between love and fear, power and trust. In your human limitations and powerlessness, the choice will be most difficult."

Logos did not hesitate in responding. "I cannot say what I shall do during that hour, Father. But it is a risk we simply cannot avoid taking if we wish to save the human race, is it not?"

The First One and Spiritus nodded their agreement, then the three set about preparing a race of people to receive the chosen one in behalf of all humanity.

And so it was that God so loved the world that he gave his only Son, that whoever believes in him may not die but may have eternal life.

One

Suffering Servant

The crucifixion of Jesus of Nazareth is one of the most certain of all historical occurrences. One might, for lack of proof, doubt the testimony of those who claim that Jesus rose from the dead, but there is no justification for doubting the death itself.

For one thing, crucifixion was not the kind of death that a group would choose to ennoble its hero. In the Roman world where this form of execution was practiced, the purpose of crucifixion was to so thoroughly humiliate the victim in public as to deter others in the community from doing what the victim had done. Generally, such extreme measures were reserved for those who had committed hideous acts. They were strung up along roadsides and near gates into cities so that people could see them and hear their cries of anguish. It was undoubtedly a gruesome sight! Many had received the customary 39 lashings, which not only streaked the skin but left welts because of lead implants in the leather of the whip. Very often, too, the victims lived for days, especially if their cross included a small peg upon which the victim could "sit" briefly to take the weight off the arms and legs. But this peg, too, eventually became a source of torment, tearing away the flesh of the buttocks so that with time the victim had no respite from pain. Death came through suffocation as the diaphragm became stifled from the prolonged drooping of the body.

If anyone wanted to know why the victim had been assigned such a horrible fate, the victim would usually be happy to explain—with his own biases, no doubt. To be certain that their own point of view in the matter was properly understood, however, the Romans affixed a sign to the cross, or hung one around the neck of the victim, detailing his wrongdoings. Although crucifixion was generally reserved for the most heinous of criminals, we know the Romans did not hesitate in crucifying hundreds and even thousands of people if they were considered subversives. This was the justification for crucifying Jesus of Nazareth. As we read in the gospels, the sign affixed to his cross stated: "This is the King of the Jews." It was by pointing out the conflict between Jesus' claims to be a king and the absolute nature of the emperor's reign that the Jewish authorities succeeded in convincing Pilate that Jesus deserved the ultimate form of torture and execution.

Unlike others who were crucified, Jesus' torture

was unique in at least two respects. First, there was the crowning of thorns, a ploy intended to mock his claims of kingship. Second, there was the spearing on the cross; the usual practice was to break the legs of the victim if they wished him to die. In addition, there was the nailing to the cross itself—an uncommon, but by no means unique, feature of Jesus' execution. The usual procedure was to tie the arms and legs of the victim, especially if they wanted to prolong his agony.

All of this adds up to an overwhelming debasement of the integrity of a human being. As we read in the scriptures, the torture and execution of Jesus provoked fear in his followers (except for those few most tenacious of lovers). The spokesman for the group denied him three times, one killed himself, and most of the others went into hiding. This was not the way they thought things would turn out. In fact, it was the *worst* of all fates! How could God have allowed such a thing to happen to the Messiah? Or was he the Messiah after all? "We were hoping that he was the one who would set Israel free," lamented the disciples on the way to Emmaus (Lk 24:21). With the crucifixion, their hopes were crushed.

Fulfillment of the Scriptures

Their experiences of the risen Lord and the Pentecost experience convinced the followers of Jesus that he was indeed the Messiah. Regarding the crucifixion, then, the primary question was one of understanding how such humiliation could have happened to God's chosen one. The general expectation was one of a political messiah, who would vanquish the foes of Israel and magnify the glory that was once David's. So strong was this expectation that it persisted even after the resurrection. "Lord, are you going to restore the rule to Israel now?" asked the disciples shortly before the ascension (Acts 1:6). In response, Jesus let them know that the time of the final restoration was known only to the Father.

It is easy to understand how the disciples, like most of the Jews of their time, could have been expecting a political messiah. In the first place, they were dissatisfied with their relationship with Rome. Although Rome had made an astounding exception in absolving them from emperor worship, the Jews were nonetheless repelled by their subservience to so pagan a presence. Then there was Pilate, who would taunt and torture. He knew the Jews well, and he despised them, often requiring them to do things that flew in the face of their most cherished beliefs. The historian Josephus recorded many instances of skirmishes between the Jews and Pilate brought about by Pilate himself. This brought him a few reprimands from Rome, which only deepened his hatred of the Jews. It was only natural that a people under political oppression should allow their hopes to take expression in the political arena.

Then there were the scriptures themselves. Many of them affirmed the coming of a glorious age, when Israel would once again be a light to all the nations. And did not the fact that the Messiah would be a descendant of David indicate that he would be a king as David—only greater? As the prophet Isaiah put it,

> On that day,
> The root of Jesse,
>   set up as a signal for the nations,
> The Gentiles shall seek out,
>   for his dwelling shall be glorious.

On that day,
The Lord shall again take it in hand
to reclaim the remnant of his people
that is left from Assyria and Egypt (Is 11:10-11).

Yet Jesus, the risen Lord and Messiah, was tortured and crucified! What was *that* all about?

It seems likely that one of the first lessons the followers of the risen one needed to learn was that their scriptures contained information about the Messiah which pointed to his suffering and death. The gospels present Jesus as telling his disciples of these matters on several occasions. But, as Luke 18:34 and similar verses state, "They understood nothing of this. His utterance remained obscure to them, and they did not grasp his meaning." We even note Peter taking Jesus aside and trying to dissuade him, which brought about one of the harshest responses attributed to Jesus. The psychological dynamics here are fairly clear: If one has strong expectations in a given area, only that which falls within the range of those expectations will be recognized. From the disciples' point of view, Jesus' miracles and the incredible magnetism of his person indicated that he might be the Messiah. It is true that there were many things he said which didn't match their expectations, but they were willing to overlook these so long as the exhibits of power continued and the crowds grew larger. Who knows but that they themselves might be given thrones! It was a happy business, something not to be spoiled with talk of torture and crucifixion by the slime of Rome. Given this backdrop, it is easy to understand why Jesus was so vague in speaking about his messianic identity.

The rigidity of the disciples' expectations was a

source of frustration for Jesus. "What little sense you have!" he tells the two on the way to Emmaus. "How slow you are to believe all that the prophets have announced! Did not the Messiah have to undergo all this so as to enter into his glory?" (Lk 24:25-26). It was a hard lesson for them to learn, but gradually they began to understand. They saw that there was much in their scriptures that they had been overlooking, things that now made sense precisely because God's Messiah had been crucified and had risen. No doubt the new life in the Spirit also had much to do with their deepening understanding.

In time we hear the passion and resurrection of Jesus proclaimed as accomplished "in fulfillment of the scriptures." Nowhere does the proclamation to Jews take place without those words. The pagans, of course, would not have appreciated this matter, but we shall examine their situation in our next chapter. The good news came first to the disciples of Jesus, who were Jews, and their first converts were also Jews. In fact, it probably never dawned on them until later that pagans could become members of the community without first becoming Jews. As we know, this was an issue which divided the early church.

The key element lacking in popular Jewish expectations of the Messiah was the recognition of the Messiah as the suffering servant of Yahweh. The clearest description of this servant is found in Isaiah 52:13—53:12. In this passage we read of a servant who was unattractive, and who was spurned by people.

Yet it was our infirmities that he bore,
　　our sufferings that he endured,
While we thought of him as stricken,
　　as one smitten by God and afflicted.

But he was pierced for our offenses,
   crushed for our sins,
Upon him was the chastisement that makes us
   whole,
   by his stripes we were healed. . . .
If he gives his life as an offering for sin,
   he shall see his descendants in a long
    life,
   and the will of the LORD shall be
   accomplished through him (Is 53:4-5,10).

We even read of a grave with sinners—an amazing prediction of the passion, death and burial of Jesus.

How was it that the suffering servant of Isaiah failed to influence Jewish expectations? We get a hint of an answer in Acts 8:26-40, in the story of Philip's confrontation with the Ethiopian eunuch. The Ethiopian, who was probably a Jewish convert, was returning home from a pilgrimage to Jerusalem. The Spirit moved Philip to catch up with his carriage, whereupon he found the Ethiopian reading about the suffering servant in the Book of Isaiah. "Tell me, if you will, of whom the prophet says this—himself or someone else?" the eunuch asks. Philip seizes the moment to explain how Jesus had died and risen "in fulfillment of the scriptures." The story ends with Philip baptizing the Ethiopian in the first stream they came to (a catechizing process which must cause the coordinators of today's R.C.I.A. programs to grimace).

It is very possible that the Jews of Jesus' time were like that Ethiopian. They either attributed the meaning to the prophet himself, or, more likely, as a reference to the sufferings of the nation as a whole.

As we know, it is very common in the Old Testament to personify the nation. It is likely that they considered the servant to be Israel—themselves—and the Messiah as the one who would deliver them from their sufferings. The suffering servant song in Isaiah 53 is not much weakened by such an interpretation, but neither does it gain much.

A clear distinction between the nation and the servant, however, appears in the second song of the servant, Isaiah 49. In this song we read that

> Now the LORD has spoken
>   who formed me as his servant from
>   the womb,
> That Jacob may be brought back to him
>   and Israel gathered to him. . . .
> It is too little, he says, for you to be
>   my servant,
>   to raise up the tribes of Jacob,
>   and restore the survivors of Israel;
> I will make you a light to the nations,
>   that my salvation may reach to the
>   ends of the earth (Is 49:5-6).

Not only will the servant redeem Israel, but he will also become a light for all the nations. The servant suffers for all, and brings the light of God to all.

We understand these words now with the aid of the Holy Spirit and the clarity of 20-20 hindsight. What we see is that the prophets were granted two glimpses of the Messiah: first, of the eventual glory of his reign, and second, of his suffering among us. Few guessed that what was glimpsed were two different aspects of his mission between which history now progresses. For the servant has come and suffered as it was written, "yet the world did not know who he was" (Jn 1:10). It is not surprising that we missed him, however. Who could have guessed that God would allow himself to be so humiliated?

---Two---

Lamb of God

The early Christian community came to understand that the crucifixion and death of Jesus had been prophesied in the Old Testament scriptures about the suffering servant of Yahweh. This helped them to identify Jesus as the Messiah in a fuller sense. He was the one whose coming had been predicted of old; his suffering, death and resurrection took place "in fulfillment of the scriptures."

But no doubt there were a few deep thinkers for whom the crucifixion provoked deeper questions. "Why was it necessary that the scriptures be fulfilled in *that* manner?" they surely asked. "Why was it necessary that the Messiah suffer and die? Why not just come among us and give us teaching, then bring it all to a glorious finale by returning to the heavens in a cloud of light? Or why not a political kingdom, from which a worldwide theocracy might be established?" These questions recognize the fact that the actions of God are not arbitrary; in fact, there are many different ways in which the story of the Messiah might have ended. Surely there must have been a reason why he was tortured and executed.

In searching for the answers to these questions, it was only natural that they again turn to their own scriptures and culture for insight. There they found two related traditions which in many ways seemed to prefigure the crucifixion. These traditions—of sacrifice and covenant—helped the early church understand what was accomplished in the crucifixion. The theology which grew from reflection on the meaning of these traditions remains very strong among Christian groups today, and still colors our explanations of the meaning of the crucifixion. Let us spend a little time, then, studying how the early church interpreted the crucifixion in the light of their traditions of sacrifice and covenant. Having done so, it will be possible for us to see if these ideas still speak to us today.

Worship and Sacrifice

The practice of offering sacrifices to God was very strong among the Jews of Jesus' time. But Judaism is not the only religion which places importance on sacrifice; almost every religion of the world includes some element of sacrifice. It was the universal nature of this phenomenon which enabled the Gentiles as well as the Jews to comprehend the meaning of the crucifixion in terms of sacrifice.

Sacrifice is a manner of worshiping God and establishing communion with him. Sacrificial worship generally includes five elements:

(1) the gift of man to the deity;   (2) the homage of the subject to the Lord;   (3) the expiation of offenses;   (4) communion with the deity in the sacrificial banquet;   (5) life released from the victim, transmitted to the deity, and conferred upon the worshipers (*Dictionary of the Bible*, John L. McKenzie, 1965).

Within Judaism, there is great diversity within each of these elements. For example, there are different kinds of gifts offered as sacrifice, depending on the kind of communion sought. Also, not all Jewish sacrifices were expiatory in nature; many were offered in thanksgiving, or in celebration of a special life event. Finally, we note that there were times when the sacrificial offering was consumed, and other times when it was not.

The practice of offering sacrifices was not confined to one's relationship with the diety. It was common practice to send gifts ahead of a visit with a higher dignitary, either to win his favor or to make amends if his favor had been lost. Sacrifice, in short, was a way of life in the ancient world, a fact which only heightened appreciation of the sacrificial dimensions of the death of Jesus.

Among the Jews (and many other groups), each element of sacrifice assumed special significance. First among the symbols was the blood, which represents life. The blood of the sacrificial animal was smeared on the altar (the symbol of the deity) or on the animal's horns. The priest, who represented the deity (and, in some circumstances, the people), then burned the sacrifice on the altar, enabling God to receive the life-blood of the animal offered in behalf of the people. Depending on the kind of sacrifice, the offering was then either eaten by all, or eaten by the priests, or completely discarded.

Of particular significance to the early Christians was the tradition of the Jewish Seder. This sacrificial meal recalled the exodus of the Jews from Egypt, and that fateful night when the avenging angel of the Lord "passed over" the homes of all whose doorposts and lintels were smeared with the blood of a lamb. Each year the Jews remember these events in their Passover celebrations, the climax of which is the meal. Like their forebears did on that first seder meal, the Jews roast and consume an unblemished lamb, whose legs are not broken. They do not paint their doorposts and lintels with the blood of the lamb, but they do solemnly read the story of the exodus, and gratefully recall the saving blood which preserved them from death.

As we know, it was during the time of the Passover that Jesus was executed. It was also at a seder meal that he offered bread and wine to his disciples as his body and blood. Although the significance of this offering was surely missed by the apostles at the time, they later came to understand the crucifixion in the light of the Passover tradition. Jesus, they saw, was the true Lamb of God who was prefigured in the Passover lamb. Just as the body and blood of the Passover lamb protected the Jews from death, so now does the blood of Christ preserve us from evil. Like the Passover lamb, Jesus was a spotless victim; unlike other crucified victims, none of his limbs was broken. And just as one partakes in some way of the life of God by consuming a sacrificial offering, so now it was possible to partake of God himself by consuming the

Body and Blood of Christ in the Lord's supper. One can only imagine the awe which the apostles experienced when they first began to see Christ in the light of their great traditions of sacrifice. It must have literally taken their breath away!

The New Covenant

The second tradition which influenced the early church's understanding of the meaning of the crucifixion was covenant. Put simply, a covenant refers to an agreement between two parties which makes special claims on both. Among the Jews of Jesus' time, there was a strong appreciation of covenant as a legally binding arrangement between people. There was also, of course, the belief that the Jews were a chosen race because they were in a covenant relationship with God. Space does not permit an exhaustive treatment of the history of the Jewish covenant relationship with God. As we did in our discussion of sacrifice, we shall here highlight only those aspects of covenant which have any bearing on the meaning of the crucifixion.

The nature of the covenant between God and Israel was understood as one of special election. It was God, after all, who initiated the relationship. It was God who helped Noah to escape the flood, then God who chose Abram and Sara and promised to make their descendants as numerous as the stars in the sky. The clearest terms of the covenant, however, were expressed during the time of Moses, and it was this understanding which persisted to the time of Jesus and even today. The formula for the covenant is summed up as follows: "You shall be my people, and I will be your God" (Jer 7:23; Ez 11:20).

Although the covenant between God and Israel existed because of God's unilateral choice, the terms of the covenant were bilateral. In return for his election and the many advantages which came to the nation as a consequence, God expected the people to be faithful to him alone. Thus the first commandment given to Moses at Sinai reads:

> "I, the LORD, am your God, who brought you out of the land of Egypt, that place of slavery. You shall not have other gods besides me. . . . For I, the LORD, your God, am a jealous God, inflicting punishment for their fathers' wickedness on the children of those who hate me, down to the third and fourth generation; but bestowing mercy down to the thousandth generation, on the children of those who love me and keep my commandments" (Ex 20:2, 5-6).

All in all it's a pretty simple agreement: God's favor for fidelity to him and his laws.

As might be expected, the ratification of the covenant at Sinai took place with a sacrificial offering. In Exodus 24 we read that Moses, having explained the laws of God to the people, sent the young men to slaughter young bulls for a peace offering. He then took half the blood from the bulls and splashed it on the altar.

> Taking the book of the covenant, he read it aloud to the people, who answered, "All that the LORD has said, we will heed and do." Then he took the blood and sprinkled it on the people, saying "This is the blood of the covenant which the LORD has made with you

in accordance with all these words of his"(Ex 24:7-8).

Through the sacrifice and the blood, the contracting parties sealed their agreement and became one blood, one family.

Following the covenant at Sinai, Jewish history featured gross violations of the terms of the contract. There were times when Israel worshiped false gods and broke the Law in many other ways. In response, God sent them prophets to remind them of their agreement. For his part, God could not go back on his word; such is his integrity that he must remain faithful. Nevertheless, the treatment received by his prophets was a source of great anger to God. Without forsaking his promise to be the God of Israel, he allowed his chosen ones to be routed in war and to go into exile (see Jer 11). Even so, we often find the Jews standing on the promises of the covenant to appeal to God for forgiveness (see Lv 26:9; Ps 25:10; Jer 14:21).

In time, the awareness began to surface that perhaps the terms of the covenant were impossible in the first place. Perhaps it was not so much that the Jews were unwilling to follow the Law; perhaps they were simply *unable* to keep their part of the deal. If that was the case, then a new covenant would have to be entered into—a different arrangement which would make for a stronger relationship between God and his chosen ones. We hear this longing expressed most clearly in Jeremiah, where he writes:

> The days are coming, says the LORD, when I will make a new covenant with the house of Israel and the house of Judah. It will not be like the covenant I made with their fathers the

41

day I took them by the hand to lead them forth from the land of Egypt; for they broke my covenant and I had to show myself their master, says the LORD. But this is the covenant which I will make with the house of Israel after those days, says the LORD. I will place my law within them, and write it upon their hearts; I will be their God, and they shall be my people. No longer will they have need to teach their friends and kinsmen how to know the LORD. All, from the least to greatest, shall know me, says the LORD, for I will forgive their evildoing and remember their sin no more (Jer 31:31-34).

In this new covenant, fidelity to the Law would not be simply a matter of external observance, but of internal as well. Obedience would not require simple conformity with external standards, but persevering fidelity to one's identity. The old covenant, then, is seen as God's way of demonstrating our need for his Spirit. The resurrection of Jesus and the coming of the Holy Spirit empowered the followers of Jesus to experience this new, interior dynamic. Time and again we read St. Paul telling his communities that external observances do no good, that it is impossible to please God by obeying the Law, and that only love fulfills the Law. Clearly the prophecy of Jeremiah was being fulfilled in the early church; the time of the new covenant had come. God would still be faithful to his chosen ones (now expanded to include all who come to him in faith—including Gentiles) and, furthermore, God would live *within* his chosen ones to help them to be faithful to their part of the deal.

What, then, of the crucifixion? It is here that we find the author of the Letter to the Hebrews expounding a theology of covenant and sacrifice that has lasted for two millenia. In chapters 8 through 10, we read of the new covenant between God and humanity, sealed through the blood of Christ.

> This is why he is mediator of a new covenant: since his death has taken place for deliverance from transgressions committed under the first covenant, those who are called may receive the promised eternal inheritance (Heb 9:15).

And just as the Sinai covenant was sealed by the sprinkling of blood, so now is the new covenant sealed by the blood of Christ (Heb 9:19-22). There is at times a barrister mentality at work in this explanation, such as the following:

> Where there is a testament, it is necessary that the death of the testator be confirmed. For a testament comes into force only in the case of death; it has no force while the testator is alive (Heb 9:16-17).

The author's main point, however, is that it is no longer necessary to offer sacrifices to God in reparation for breaches in the old covenant. With Jesus' sacrificial death and resurrection, humanity has entered into a new covenant with God. If one needs any favors from God, one need only appeal to Jesus, who is seated at the right hand of the Father, where he constantly makes intercession for us as the high priest par excellence (Heb 7:26—8:6).

Today's Situation
I can imagine that it must have been a powerful experience for the first Jewish and Gentile converts to

recognize in the crucifixion of Christ the fulfillment of their long traditions of sacrifice. I often wonder, however, if these concepts still speak to us today. Many times while teaching on these topics, I have noted that familiar glazing over of the eyes which indicates that my audience is simply not with me. And small wonder! We do not live in a world where sacrifice is practiced as in days of old. Nor do we seal our covenants with the sprinkling of blood. What we have been doing for centuries, then, is presenting a theology of the crucifixion in terms of what it meant to the early Christians. And while it is certainly intriguing to see in Jesus the fulfillment of the Passover sacrifice, or to regard the Lord's supper as the new Seder, I wonder if it is meaningful to today's people.

Could it be that our alienation from the ancient traditions of sacrifice and covenant are accounting for such perverted theologies of the crucifixion as we find in many places today? In some of these explanations, God comes off looking like an angry, vindictive beast who requires killing and blood for his appeasement. Yet that, as we have seen, was not how the Jews understood sacrifice. And the new covenant theology had nothing to do with vindication, but with establishing a new, interior relationship between God and humanity.

In short, do we really know what we are talking about today when we speak of Jesus as the Lamb of God who takes away the sins of the world? Does the phrase, "washed in the blood of the Lamb," mean today what it did when the first Christians rejoiced in the ultimate sacrifice of the Son? I think not. Furthermore, I believe our evangelical successes are being diminished because of our attempts to explain the meaning of the crucifixion primarily in reference to examples that are no longer relevant to today's people.

Lest I be misunderstood here, I am certainly not saying that our attempts to explain the crucifixion in terms of sacrifice and covenant are a complete waste of time. If nothing else, it is good to know how the first Christians understood *their* faith. So let us, by all means, continue with these teachings. And let us continue to study the scriptures that we may gain an appreciation of the meaning of sacrifice and covenant. Let us have our parish seder meals to help us better understand the Lord's supper and the implications of the new covenant. But let us also expand our teachings about the crucifixion and the Eucharist to include other models as well. This will be the concern of future chapters.

_____Three_____

Prince of Peace

The early church viewed the crucifixion as having taken place in fulfillment of the scriptures, bringing to completion the traditions of sacrifice that had characterized its worship, and sealing a new covenant between humanity and God. There is yet another body of reflection on the meaning of the crucifixion intermingling with these themes. In this third view, Jesus is seen as the Prince of Peace who has come to overthrow the prince of this world. "It was to destroy the devil's works that the Son of God revealed himself," concludes 1 John 3:8. Virtually every book of the New Testament carries this theme.

There is much gallantry and adventure in this salvation metaphor. If we were to give it a title, we might call it a "A Tale of Two Kingdoms." (In the *Spiritual Exercises*, St. Ignatius has a "Meditation on the Two Standards.") On the one hand there is the kingdom of Satan, covering the world in darkness and attempting to lead the human race away from God into its own self-destruction. But the kingdom of God will not stand idly by and watch this tragedy unfold. God fights back by calling out a people and teaching them the Law. He also promises a messiah, who will break the hold of Satan and bring a return of the captives from the imprisonment of the enemy. Jesus' message is clear: "The kingdom of God is now among you." His power is greater than Satan's, so he casts out demons wherever he goes. In the end, however, he renounces his power and allows himself to be taken hostage by the servants of the enemy. He is tortured and executed, but emerges on the other side, risen and glorious. The crucifixion, which appeared to be the enemy's victory, turns out to be Christ's victory march. This is the stuff of great drama; in fact, most of the great dramatic tales of the world are patterned along these lines: bad guys versus good guys, and the conquest of virtue over wickedness.

An issue which has arisen in our day—especially among those of a liberal theological bent—is whether or not "A Tale of Two Kingdoms" is merely a story, or if it describes a real confrontation between God and evil spirits. No one doubts the fact of evil, and that evil is an immense power in our world. But do we need a devil to explain the origins of evil? Is all this talk of the devil in the New Testament merely symbolic, and culturally limited? Are there any implications here relative to the meaning of the crucifixion? Let us spend some time reflecting on these questions.

Demons and Demonology

Belief in demons is a fairly universal phenomenon, a fact which undoubtedly helped the early Christian preachers explain the meaning of the crucifixion to their Gentile converts. We note, however, that early Judaism spoke little about devils and evil spirits, even though their neighbors all accepted evil spirits as a fact of life. The traditional view that the tempting serpent in Eden was none other than Satan did not belong to early Judaism. No doubt it was the strict monotheism of the Jews which prevented them from accepting the existence of evil spirits who were determined to frustrate the designs of God.

Between 538 and 331 B.C., however, Israel belonged to the Persian empire. The religion of the Persians was Zoroastrianism, which must have intrigued the Jews in many ways. In contrast to the polytheism of his time, Zoroaster had taught that there was one God, Ahura Mazda ("Wise Lord"), who created and ruled the earth. Humanity had turned away from Ahura Mazda due to the tempting influences of evil spirits under the dominion of their powerful leader, Ahriman. Good spirits dispatched by Ahura Mazda continually did battle with the demons, but the ultimate salvation of the human race would come through a savior born of a virgin. Zoroaster conceived of an eternal, blissful afterlife, but only after the soul was purified through a purgatory of fire. A final judgment and bodily resurrection would conclusively demonstrate Ahura Mazda's victory over evil.

From Zoroastrianism, the Jews adopted the view that evil ultimately derives from spirits in opposition to God. The danger here is that we humans will be let "off the hook" for our role in the perpetuation of evil, but Judaism did not go this far. Evil spirits were viewed as a tremendous nuisance, but they were nonetheless subject to the commands of God. In the Book of Job, for example, Satan appears in the courts of heaven, where he receives permission from God to test Job. This represents the popular view of that time that Satan's work is primarily one of tempting, or accusing. We hear something of this in Jesus' warning to Peter that Satan has asked to sift him like wheat (Lk 22:31).

The years of contact between the Jews and the Greeks beginning in the fourth century B.C. further influenced Jewish thinking about evil spirits. The Greek word for spirits (both good and bad) is *daimon*, which we recognize as the root of our English word, demon. Those spirits that were bad were called *diabolos*, or diabolical. Because of their reverence for philosophy and wisdom, the Greeks viewed the work of evil spirits as one of distorting the truth. They were slanderous, liars, "the Father of lies," as Jesus called Satan, the chief among the diabolos daimons (Jn 8:44).

During the time of Christ, then, the influences of Zoroastrianism and Greek cosmology had stimulated among Jews the widespread belief that armies of demons wreaked great havoc among human beings in their efforts to frustrate the plans of God. The leader of these demons was called Satan (also Beelzebub, Belial, Asmodeus, Sammael, Mastemah and Apollyon; the name Lucifer is owed to a misinterpretation of Isaiah 14:12-15). These evil spirits were blamed for mental and physical illnesses, wicked actions among people, and even crop failures and weather patterns. If one were to successfully recover from a malady, the influence of the evil spirit would have to be dealt with. Thus the ministry of exorcism came to be an essential practice in praying with the sick for their recovery; we know from Matthew 12:27 and other verses that Jewish exorcisms must have been a common affair.

Into the Enemy's Camp

It was into this Jewish world of evil spirits and exorcisms that Jesus of Nazareth came to live. From the first, there were evil powers at work to destroy him. Herod wanted him killed, but an angel intervened and urged Joseph to flee the countryside. After this slight brush with the Evil One, things settled down a bit. No doubt Jesus was being watched during the hidden years in Nazareth, but the Evil One was waiting for the right moment. What good would it do to crush the Messiah when no one even knew him for who he was?

After the baptism by John, the confrontation began. Jesus went into the desert, where, after a long period of fasting, he was weak and vulnerable. The Evil One tried to persuade him to define his ministry in terms of pleasure, power and security, but Jesus recognized the trap and dismissed him. "Away with you, Satan!" he commanded. "You shall do homage to the Lord your God; him alone shall you adore."

Satan was not finished with him, however. If he could not convince Jesus to opt for an earthly kingdom, then maybe the people could force his hand. The people were expecting a political messiah, so Jesus was very careful about creating false hopes. But true to their nature, the evil spirits tried to frustrate Jesus' strategy. When Jesus commanded them to leave

their victims, they had to obey, for he was the One.
They could shriek, however, and complain, and tell
the people who he was. This strategy seemed to
work, for it stirred up the people and increased Jesus'
prestige. They even managed to infiltrate into the
ranks of his disciples, working through Simon to persuade him to renounce his mission. Jesus recognized
the ploy and rebuked this diabolical work through Simon. It appeared that there was no stopping him.

Onward he went in his ministry, much to Satan's
chagrin. He would not stop to fight, nor would he allow himself to become an earthly king, which would
only play into Satan's hands. What he was up to Satan could not guess, but surely it spelled trouble for
the dark kingdom. As long as he held onto his power,
however, Satan could not touch him.

Then came that fateful Passover, and Satan could
not believe his good fortune. One of the disciples—Judas, from the inner group—had agreed with Satan
that Jesus should go for an earthly kingdom. Jesus
knew all about it, of course, but he seemed to do
nothing to oppose Judas' plans. Furthermore, he did
not seem to have his power, for Satan's ever-vigilant
eye of malice could now see into his heart. And what
he saw was anguish, uncertainty and a fear of suffering and dying. Who would have believed it? Oh,
there was still that dreadful connection with the One,
but even that seemed weak and tenuous. "Never
mind it!" Satan decides. "If he will not be an earthly
king, then let him die and begone—back to heaven if
he must, but at least away from the earth."

"Now is the hour of darkness," says the Christ to
his apostles.

"Amen!" exults Satan.

It was easy to mobilize the Jewish and Roman authorities. They had long ago decided that there were more important concerns in the world than love, so it was possible to get them to rationalize anything. "This character Jesus will bring the Romans down on you and prevent you from worshiping your God," spoke Satan to the Jews. The Jews responded by arresting him, trying him for blasphemy, and deciding to have him crucified. Now for Pilate: "Any more trouble with these Jews and Tiberius will have you sent away," whispered Satan. Although convinced of Jesus' innocence, Pilate compromised himself and gave Jesus up for crucifixion.

With great jubilation, Satan watched as Jesus was tortured and mocked. The torturers found themselves gripped by depths of malice they seldom experienced. They lashed him with special relish, and they spit on him and mocked him as though he were trash. The crowd who watched him carry the cross jeered merrily. "See what happens to the good and holy!" they sneered.

A terrible thought then struck Satan: What if he would go through with it until near the end, then reclaim his power and come down from the cross? This would prove conclusively that he was the One, would it not? It would prove that any attempts to mock him or kill him would be thwarted in the end. "He must not come down!" Satan concluded. "I'll have to set it up as a dare—use a bit of reverse psychology to keep him up there," he decides.

A nearby observer is prompted to say, "If you really are the Son of God, come down from that cross! Surely you will not let the Evil One put you to death?"

It works! He only hangs there, his life trickling away. Soon he will be dead, and it will be back to old times. A couple of generations and his teachings will be twisted so that no one will know what he said and what he meant. How stupid are the earthlings! And how stupid God, too! If only he had enough sense to listen to the smartest of his angels. . . .

He just hangs there—a human-like creature dying as if he *were* a human. What a travesty?! In one last effort, he offers himself to his Father and gives up his ghost. What a pathetic creature! The few who followed him are devastated; they'll be easy targets later, when love's grief can be turned into cynicism and despair. Now is the time to return to the pit, to hold a great council to discuss this strange matter and plot future strategy.

Satan enters his realm and is shocked to discover several of his chief demons fleeing in a panic. "The One! The One!" they shout. Yet how could that be? Sheol is for *humans*, and he was the One. Surely the One was not *really* a human being! Satan approaches, but cannot enter his own domain, for the sight of Jesus disgusts him. He can only stand outside the pit, wailing and gnashing his teeth as he listens to Jesus speaking to the prisoners.

Inside, Jesus speaks of the beginning of a new age, when God himself will make his home in the hearts of humans. He speaks of the power of the Spirit, helping humans to conquer evil. He then turns to the walls of Sheol and begins walking toward the immense gate with its legion of guards. As he walks, many of the prisoners follow after him, although many fly in the opposite direction. Gazing into his dark stronghold out of the corner of his eye, Satan sees the light within Jesus growing in intensity. The legion at the gate flee as he approaches, leaving the gate unguarded. Standing before the gate, Jesus then lifts his hands and the chains fall to the ground. Slowly the gate opens, admitting the entrance of a light so warm and intense that Satan must flee in horror. His stronghold is ruined: The prisoners have been set free, although a few have run to darker corners. Still, there are only corners now: no more enclosures. If he had known it would have turned out like this, he would never have allowed Jesus to die. Yet who would have thought that *God* would have come to Sheol as a *human being*! And who would have thought that he would lead the dreadful human slime out with his own light!

Never mind! Time to get back to earth to keep the secret from getting out! Got to make sure no one knows he's alive. The tomb: It must be guarded!

Returning to Jerusalem, Satan finds that the Jewish authorities have already anticipated this trouble. There is a good, solid guard posted at the tomb, and the gravestone is sealed properly. The prisoners in Sheol have been freed, but it will do the earthlings no good unless they learn about it. Only if someone were to rise from the dead could they guess at the truth. Then it would surely be the end! There could be work toward the damnation of individuals and maybe even a few nations, but that would bring little satisfaction in the long run. "Maybe I will have to take possession of a human myself!" he admits aloud. The thought of it makes him retch with disgust. No time to dwell on such dreadful options now, he soon decides—not so long as the tomb remains closed.

Sharing the Good News

I don't know, do people still believe in the devil? Fundamentalists do, and so do people involved in the charismatic renewal. Most liberal theologians do not (although they believe in evil as a greater-than-human power); neither do scientific materialists and secular humanists. Spiritual directors using the exercises of St. Ignatius of Loyola are aware of the darkness that proceeds from the angel of light; other counselors—of psychological and pastoral bent—tend to root evil in human ignorance and irresponsibility.

Among religious educators, there seem to be two extremes. First are the liberal theologians, who in their efforts to demythologize the scriptures point to the influence of the Persians and the Greeks in contributing to the widespread belief in demons that existed during the time of Christ. The assumption here is that because belief in demons was stimulated by contact with non-Jewish cultures, this somehow diminishes its authenticity as revealed truth. In this view, Jesus is seen as a man of his culture who believes in demons because that's what he was taught, and who casts them out because the sick would not have believed they were really healed unless some sort of exorcism was performed (much as today's sick do not believe the doctor has really ministered to them unless drugs are prescribed). The second extreme trivializes belief in the devil by exaggerating the influence of the evil spirit. This extreme would include those who see a devil behind every slight deviation from the "straight and narrow," thereby minimizing the role of human responsibility in the perpetuation of evil. Demon enthusiasts are also prone to reduce human history to a struggle between God and

Satan, with humanity simply caught in the middle, a view which easily disintegrates into dualism.

As with all things, the truth is probably somewhere between the extremes, and this is where the church's teachings seem to point. In response to the demythologizers, we might say that non-Jewish cultures contributed tremendously to the Jews' understanding of God and his workings in creation. If we were to disregard everything that was not purely Jewish in origin, we would have little left in the scriptures. Then there is the teaching of Christ himself: There can be no doubt that *he* believed in demons as personal spirits intent on subverting the reign of God. To say that he was merely a man of his culture on this point is to forget that Jesus deviated from cultural norms in many areas, including the observance of Sabbath laws and the treatment of women and children. If there were really no such things as devils—if the power of evil was instead a kind of spiritual sewage accumulating as a consequence of human sinfulness—then is it not likely that Jesus would have known about it? Is it not likely that he would have taught us differently if there were no devils?

On the other hand, devil enthusiasts often seem to forget that the devil has not been given permission to overwhelm human will power. The traditional teaching on devils holds that Satan's primary role lies in *tempting* humans to stray from love and truth. Even in cases of partial and complete possession, the human will is free to cooperate with or reject the demon; the ministries of deliverance and exorcism could not succeed if this were not so. Although Jesus believed in the devil, he did not spend a great deal of time on this subject. He took the devil seriously, but he never focused on it except in rebuke when it was blocking someone's ability to grow in love. For an excellent review of the powers and limitations of evil spirits, I recommend *The Theology of Christian Perfection* by Antonio Royo, O.P., and Jordan Aumann, O.P. (Priory Press, 1962).

I believe there is great promise in explaining the crucifixion as the means by which God broke the hold of Satan in our world. As I have already let on in the prologue and in this chapter, I believe the fall of our first parents left humanity especially vulnerable to the influence of Satan. This is why Jesus referred to Satan as the prince of this world (Jn 12:31; 14:30; 16:11). The incarnation, then, can be viewed as a rescue mission by God to free humanity from the treachery of Satan. In the best of spy-thriller traditions, God allows himself to be taken captive by the enemy, but only to enter his camp. Satan is elated, because he believes the crucifixion will put an end to the ministry of the Messiah. Satan's mistake was in denying the humanity of Christ; so intense is his hatred and loathing of humanity that it seemed inconceivable that a higher being would empty itself to become truly human. Satan sees Jesus as God in a human body, and believes that Christ's primary mission is as teacher and exorcist—thus the passion of Satan to put an end to his ministry, or to get Jesus focused in on worldly issues. It is because he is truly human, however, that Jesus goes the way of all the dead to Sheol, that Limbo of sorts where the souls of the dead were prevented from going to heaven because of their fallen nature. But Jesus is not only human, he is also divine. Thus he is able to pass through Sheol as he returns to his Father; those good-natured souls who wish to follow in the way of the God-man will also be saved. Because of Christ's crucifixion, death and descent into Sheol (which is different from hell), Satan's hold is broken. Suffering and death are taken up into new life with Christ, and the way to eternal life now passes straight through the enemy's camp.

I find this explanation of the meaning of the crucifixion to be immensely exciting! In the first place, it is entirely faithful to scripture and tradition. Secondly, I think it provides a powerful testimony to the love of God. In the light of this story, I can understand how Christ's death saved *me* from sin. I see, too, that there is nothing in this rescue mission which points to a vindictive God who demands a human sacrifice for the appeasement of his just wrath. What stands out is the *love* of God, and how this love for humanity was so intense that it emptied itself to become as we are so that we might become as God is. Let's teach this message in our religion classes, and let's hear it proclaimed from the pulpit: *By his crucifixion and death, the Prince of Peace has freed us from the snares of the prince of this world.*

My belief in Christ's victory over Satan has kept me sane during those several times in my life when I have felt attacked by the powers of darkness. These attacks seem to come most frequently when I am directing a retreat. At some point during the weekend, I become nearly overwhelmed with negativity—toward myself, the retreatants, the staff I am working with, and anything else! During those times it is as though every negative thought and feeling I have experienced during the retreat somehow coalesces to form a gigantic eruption of self-hate and revulsion for others. Frequently this will happen in the middle of the night, when I'm trying to rest up for the next day; the insomnia only adds to my hatred. There's only one way to overcome this darkness, and that's by turning my attention fully toward the Lord. Recalling that he has broken the power of the enemy is a great consolation to me. Eventually, he leads me through the enemy's camp into new depths of love for him, for myself and for others. How pathetic the darkness seems in contrast! How real is God's love in comparison! So energized am I from these rescue missions that I don't even seem to miss those couple of hours of sleep the next day. Amazing!

Four

Immanuel

During the past seven years, I have learned much about sin and redemption by working to help alcoholics and drug addicts find their way back to health. Before I had much training and experience in this work, it seemed to me that the most important thing would be to keep them from continuing to use these destructive chemicals. This is important, of course, for there can be no hope for recovery as long as they continue using. But keeping chemicals out of one's digestive system is only a first step in getting well; the consequences of chemical use must be addressed as well. The body has been hurt; self-hating attitudes predominate; broken relationships abound; illegal and immoral acts litter the past. If abstaining from chemicals is the only thing one does, there is a strong likelihood that negative consequences will continue to accumulate.

61

The dynamics of chemical dependency can teach us much about the fall and redemption. By saying no to God's terms for relationship, our first parents said yes to the devil (just as by saying yes to emotional stimulation by chemicals, there is a no to natural sources of stimulation). After this disobedience, the intimacy which had characterized God's relationship with humanity became contaminated with the presence of Satan. Lacking a full awareness of God's loving presence, our first parents became fearful, for fear is the psychological consequence of the absence of love (1 Jn 4:18). This fear spawned thoughts of self-concern, which consequently twisted the human will to become self-seeking. Thus it was that human beings, who were created to know and serve love, became selfish and fearful as a result of the fall.

It didn't take long before human selfishness began to affect the entire creation. As the story of Cain and Abel reveals, human relationships deteriorated. The story of Sodom and Gomorrah further illustrates the corruption that took place in human nature. In time, human selfishness began to affect the innocent creation, as we pillaged and plundered and destroyed our planet without regard for our long-term interests. The natural and logical consequences of this selfishness have led us to a point in history where the very survival of our planet is at stake. If we don't destroy our world with nuclear weapons, then we must nonetheless contend with pollution and the "greenhouse effect" of warming the atmosphere, which could cause the oceans to rise and destroy many of our coastal cities.

When we speak of sin, then, we speak of a power that moves us to destruction on all levels; this is the

Judeo-Christian insight into the problem of evil. In contrast with other explanations of evil, the Judeo-Christian tradition maintains that there is a distortion in the human will which sabotages even our most noble strivings (see Rom 7:13-25). This distortion is the presence of sin in our very nature. Because sin is the dark power of the Evil One, anyone who sins belongs to the devil (1 Jn 3:8). This darkness, however, which ultimately derives from Satan, has contaminated human nature and the human environment. Thus it is that we speak of sin as originating in the world, the flesh and the devil.

In Chapter 3 we discussed the manner in which the death and resurrection of Jesus of Nazareth overcame the power of the devil. The influence of the devil in today's world remains, to be sure, but its decisive hold has been broken. The gates of Sheol have been opened, and there now exists the *possibility* of a full relationship with God through Christ. But what about the other two power centers of sin—the flesh and the world? If these centers are not also transformed, then we shall be like the alcoholic who has only stopped drinking; he still lives with the illness in his mind and flesh, and he continually meets hostility from the people who have been affected by his illness. In this analogy, the victory over the prince of this world is like abstinence from alcohol: It is a necessary first step toward healing and reconciliation. It is only a first step, however, for the other power centers of sin must be dealt with as well.

In this chapter we will reflect upon the crucifixion as the means by which Christ broke the power of sin in our human nature. Chapter 5 will examine the crucifixion and the sin of the world.

Fallen Human Nature

With the fall came the loss of intimacy with God and the consequent darkness of fear in the human soul. The human spirit, which was created in God's image and likeness, continues to yearn for the fullness of life which only God can satisfy, but on every front this yearning seems to be frustrated. A typical compensation is to build psychological defenses between ourselves and reality so that we will not be overwhelmed by our fears. It is, in part, about this system of defenses that scripture speaks when referring to "the flesh."

One of the first defenses we build concerns our attitudes about death. In the absence of intimacy with God, death looms on the horizon of consciousness as the ultimate denial of our identity. As Ernest Becker described so powerfully in his Pulitzer Prize winning book, *The Denial of Death*, the very roots of what we call personality derive from our attempts to define ourselves in the face of death. Much of this kind of self-affirmation is spent in denying our corruptibility, as evidenced by our preoccupation with staying young. But what is the alternative? Who wants to admit the inevitability of his or her death? Who wants to dwell on the absurdity of a death-bracketed life?

A further compensation for our gut-level fear of life and death is selfishness. If, after all, the end of life is death, then doesn't it make sense to spend one's days eating, drinking and making merry? If death is the end, then the logical thing to do in this life is to seek pleasure, status, power and security. After all, we might as well enjoy ourselves along the way, right? In time, these pursuits can become so strong as to take on a more or less autonomous manner of functioning in the will. We forget (or maybe we never knew) that the reason we chose this life stance is because we are trying to fill up the emptiness whose name is fear.

It doesn't work, however. Pleasure, status, power and security are only short-term gratifications whose attainment only leaves us thirsting for more. But what is *more*? Is not our perpetual yearning for more precisely the curse of fallen humanity? We hunger for a meaning in life that can satisfy our deepest appetites, but nowhere is this meaning to be found—or so it seems. We erect philosophies in an attempt to identify life's meaning, but one person's meaning is another's heresy. Who's to say who's right when it comes to meaning? Who can reveal to us a truth that salvages meaning in the face of death?

Fear, selfishness and meaninglessness conspire to aggravate the natural corruptibility that is already part of our nature. It is no secret that negative attitudes produce negative consequences in the body. Many health professionals today claim that excessive stress is our number one health problem—contributing to heart diseases, ulcers and cancers. That life brings a natural suffering due to aging and death is already bad enough; that we add more suffering because of our negative attitudes only makes things worse. But awareness of our capacity for self-induced suffering only seems to increase our cynicism and self-loathing. Quite a predicament we find ourselves in on planet earth!

We have made numerous responses in our attempts to cope with these miserable realities, however. One response has been to erect a system of laws that serve to discourage behaviors injurious to the well-being of the community. Such a system of laws characterized the covenant at Sinai, where God revealed his laws to humanity through Moses. While there can be no doubt that laws have helped to improve the quality of human life, there is nonetheless a sense in which laws also make us worse than before. This is especially true with regard to God's laws, for the plain fact is that no one is capable of keeping God's laws all the time. When we break these laws, then, we are guilty of an injustice which only God can forgive. So long as we are not forgiven, we live in guilt, which only adds to the negativity already festering in our minds.

The ultimate injustice, however, and one of which we are all aware, is that we do not function as we were created to function. God created us to know, love and serve him in this world, and to be happy with him forever in eternity, but we are usually about a different business. There is a deep-down guilt which cannot be shaken because it derives from the very roots of our nature, where, if we are the least bit reflective, we know ourselves to be children of God who have gone awry. Yes, we are children in rebellion, although we may not have ever chosen to put ourselves in this position. We are born this way, and our fallen cultures with their various traditions of selfishness only deepen our darkness. What an affront to God this is! An analogy on the human level would be that despite our best efforts at parenting, our children nonetheless decided to live as swine.

These, then, are the sorry consequences of our fall from intimacy with God: fear of life and death; selfish pursuits of pleasure, status, power and security; a sense of the meaninglessness of life in the face of suffering and death; guilt because of our awareness that we are not as we should be. These are the stains of original sin which are experienced by all who are descendants of our fallen ancestors. To be sure, Satan works tirelessly to keep these fires stirred up within us. But even if there were no devil, the power center of sin in our fallen nature would continue to keep us alienated from God. That is why it was necessary that the Messiah not only break the hold of Satan, but also put to death the hold of sin in the flesh.

Redemption of the Flesh

The unredeemed, fallen person is trapped inside himself or herself—a victim of fears, selfishness, guilt and cynicism. Such a person is incapable of true intimacy with others, and so has become like the devil, a creature whose relationships are characterized by fear and manipulative control. Escaping this trap is very difficult, for the power of sin is continually making a claim on the human soul (Rom 7:19-23). Only love can break these chains; to the extent that we love and are loved, we will be free.

The love of other human beings can go a long way toward redeeming us. Because of our love for others, we become willing to face our fears, and to do battle with our selfishness for their sake. In loving we allow others entry into our lives and thus find some measure of intimacy. We learn that we are not alone, and this in itself is a great healing experience.

But human love cannot touch those deep-down places where fear has its stronghold within us. Indeed, it often seems that our best human loves serve only to make us more acutely aware of that deeper love and intimacy we so desperately need. Nor can human love provide satisfactory compensation for our fear of death. On a purely human level, the best we can do is to love one another and share our fears with one another. This helps, but it does not thoroughly satisfy.

It is the death and resurrection of Jesus of Nazareth which broke the hold of sin in the human flesh. How did he do this for us? Let us reflect awhile on this question.

First, Jesus provides teaching about life, morality and the kingdom of God. This ministry of teaching helps to dispel the darkness of sin in the human mind. By meditating on his teachings we begin to perceive truth and light, and this helps us to recognize a new meaning in life.

Second, Jesus comes to us as a healer of broken bodies and souls. It was not enough simply to teach. He also revealed God's unambiguous love for us by touching and healing on many occasions. "It is my Father's will that you become whole," this ministry seems to say. The corruptibility of the flesh which resulted from loss of intimacy with God is healed when the touch of Christ brings the life of God into the soul.

Third, the suffering and death of Jesus demonstrates that God is in solidarity with the human condition. By suffering and dying as we do, Jesus is Immanuel (literally, "God is with us"). No longer may we say that suffering and death are meaningless if the feet of God have passed that way. If we find the empathy of another to be consoling during our times of tribulation, then how much more the empathy of God himself! "For we do not have a high priest who is unable to sympathize with our weakness, but one who was tempted in every way that we are, yet never sinned" (Heb 4:15).

This solidarity of God would almost be sufficient to redeem us from the sin of the flesh, but there is more—and this is the difficult part to comprehend. In 2 Corinthians 5:21, we read that Jesus, through his suffering and death, took our sins upon himself and *became sin*, "so that we might become the very holiness of God." There's something great and mysterious going on here, but how are we to understand it? How can it be that Christ, who was sinless, became sin?

This is the way I understand it. I have noted that during times in my life when I am close to God, I am also more acutely aware of the hurt and anguish of another. If we spend a bit of time together talking things out, I feel as though the person's turmoil has entered into my own soul and become part of me. But God's grace is such that through prayer and loving discipline I am able to continue on my own journey and eventually become transformed myself as I grow out of this turmoil. As for the other person, it seems as though this sharing between us has diminished his or her experience of darkness. In some real but mysterious way, empathic loving leads to transformation for both parties.

Because what I mean by "empathic loving" could easily be misconstrued, let me make it clear at this point that I am not talking about taking on the problems of others *for* them. There is a kind of empathy that makes both parties worse off than before. In fact, I do not think that it is even a good idea to make it a goal to seek to experience the troubles of others. The only Christian goal is loving, and loving people will find more than enough opportunities to share their burdens. Note, however, that Christ is not only empathic lover, but also teacher and healer; while sharing our burdens with us, he also helps us to find our way out of our troubles so that we can walk in greater freedom.

Because of what I have learned through my experiences in compassionate loving, I believe I have a better understanding of what we mean when we say that Christ became sin. His heart was sinless, and he was ever in communion with the Father. Where we knew mostly darkness and fear in the depths of our being, he knew only light and love. But his is a love which embraces us totally. His is a heart which is forever open to receiving from us the totality of our experiences, and this includes our fear and darkness. Because in his inner being Christ is filled with love and light, he is also capable of totally feeling our fear and darkness. This, it seems, is what happened to him during his passion and death. All throughout his public ministry he had been the empathic lover and, hence, the wounded healer. During the time of his passion, however, his heart was opened to experience fully the darkness and fears of *all* of humanity. He whose heart loved and embraced all at that moment experienced the power of sin as it corrupts all of humanity. Love opened itself totally to fear that it might conquer fear, but the consequences of this loving crushed the man Jesus. He sweated blood, and cried out to his Father for a return of sweetness and light. He asked for a change of plans—maybe a return to teaching and healing—but the darkness only seemed to grow stronger. Finally, as the executioners approached, he accepted his cup and in that surrender regained his peace. The man Jesus who surrendered to his torturers and who now carried in his soul the darkness of all humanity had become sin itself, and it

was thus that he accepted torture, ridicule and crucifixion.

Because of his suffering and death, Jesus has
changed everything. By totally identifying himself
with us in our darkness, he opened for us the possibility of intimacy with God. He has plumbed the
depths of our existence so completely that nowhere
can we go within ourselves and not find him waiting
for us. The fear that once spawned the power of sin
in the flesh has been touched with love and only
needs now our cooperation in love for its complete
transformation. Even death itself has been changed. If
God lives in Christ and Christ has died, then it follows that death itself now belongs to God, and God is
experienced in death. Death no longer leads to Sheol
for those who die in Christ, but to God himself. The
old strongholds of fear and death have been totally
routed.

There is one final matter to be considered, however, and this has to do with guilt and forgiveness.
We considered earlier the injustice of human beings
breaking God's laws, and of living short of the ideals
to which love calls us. This injustice only God can forgive, for it is an offense against God himself. As long
as we are not forgiven by God, there will remain in us
a sense of guilt which holds the power of sin in our
souls.

In the crucifixion of Christ, we encounter this forgiveness of God. As he hung on the cross, Christ
gazed down at his executioners and saw malicious
jeering and hatred. He saw children of Satan who
had lost their way, and he grieved to see the distortion that sin had brought to our nature. True justice
would require that humanity be allowed to suffer the

consequences of its sinfulness. But if humanity was to be set free, something more than justice would be required. Then came those wonderful, liberating words, which must have astonished those who stood by the cross: "Father forgive them, for they know not what they are doing."

Forgiveness! And forgiveness extended by the Son—God himself, the only one who can extend such a reprieve. The strict demands of justice are lifted for those who will accept this undeserved gift. Existential guilt is dissolved in mercy and pardon. The final bastion of sin in the flesh is swallowed up by love. The redemption is complete. A new way to live is opened before us. Nothing can separate us from the love of God extended by Christ Jesus through his death and resurrection.

Sharing the Good News

What we have been reflecting upon in this chapter is original sin, and the manner in which the death and resurrection of Jesus Christ has freed us from its hold. The approach we have taken is quite different from the one I was taught as a child, however.

Traditionally, we have explained original sin and redemption in juridical terms: Disobeying God is an injustice which warrants fatal consequences; Christ accepts the consequences for us, thus dying in our place; the ransom is paid; the gates of heaven are now opened. While this forensic metaphor of substitutionary atonement may be theologically valid, I must say, as I've indicated before, that it leaves me unmoved and very much confused about God's loving nature. I have also interviewed many others about the crucifixion during the course of writing this book, and have learned that most people do not understand how Christ's passion and death saved them from sin. They piously recited back to me the usual forensic formula, but when pressed to share the meaning they derived from this teaching, they usually could not do so. The prevailing attitude among many seems to be that Christ died for us, and it is enough simply to accept this truth and leave it at that. Understanding precisely *how* this sacrifice has saved us from our sins is impossible, for we are dealing here with mysteries beyond the grasp of the human mind.

I disagree with these objections, of course. The problem, as I see it, is not that we are dealing here with mysteries that cannot be understood, but that we have been given a teaching that does not make very much sense to us. Thus the old explanations of substitutionary atonement are, for many of us, irrelevant and meaningless. But I believe that God passionately desires that we understand and appreciate the reconciliation that has taken place through the crucifixion, for this was the ultimate expression of his love for us.

The explanation of the fall and redemption presented in this chapter (and in many other writings) might be called the "intimacy metaphor." In this explanation, special emphasis is placed on the loss of intimacy with God which resulted from the fall, and how the consequent fear in our hearts led us to selfishness. The mission of Christ, then, becomes one of restoring intimacy between God and humanity through empathic loving. Through the incarnation, God enters fully into our nature that we might once again be able to enter fully into his. Because his heart is perfectly loving, Christ is able to empathize completely with our inner darkness, accepting it in his own person and bearing it unto transformation. We learn that even while we are in the darkness of sin, God still loves and forgives us completely.

What I like most about the intimacy metaphor is that it seems, more than the old forensic explanations, to emphasize the love of God for humanity. I believe the forensic metaphor—with its talk of ransom, sacrificial victim, expiation, satisfaction and substitutionary atonement—often leaves people confused about God's loving nature. This was my problem in the past, and I find it to be an impediment to appreciating God's love among many today. If there are any absolutes in Christianity, God's love for humanity is one. Therefore, we should make every attempt to explain the works of God in a manner that helps people to appreciate his love for us. If the forensic metaphor is a block to such appreciation, then perhaps we should not use it any more, especially if there are better ways to explain things.

A final advantage of the intimacy metaphor is that it holds great promise in helping both religious and secular-minded people to understand the mission of Christ. There are many people today, for example, who do not believe in the fall, but who view the human condition as but a natural consequence of where we are in our evolutionary history. For such people— and they are many, both within and without the church—the traditional explanations of redemption, which were all premised on the fall, mean very little. What, after all, is the point of talking about the crucifixion as a corrective to the fall if one does not believe in the fall in the first place? But we all know fear, selfishness and guilt in our lives, and we all struggle with the meaning of life in the face of death. We may not identify these negative forces as a consequence of original sin, but they are real nonetheless. Yet there is something within us that longs for intimacy—with other people, with creation, and with a higher dimension of life. Indeed, the expectation of intimacy in relationships is stronger today than ever before; it is because this expectation so frequently meets with disappointment that more separations and divorces in marriage are taking place (whereas, in decades past, one or both parties—not holding to their "right" to intimacy—would have just hung in there to honor their part in the "contract" of marriage). If we reflect a little, we will see that it is our fear of rejection and our selfishness which frustrate our struggles in intimacy.

The good news for believers and nonbelievers is this: *Intimacy is possible* because the love of Christ has already embraced our fears and overcome them; *forgiveness from guilt is now possible* because Christ has forgiven us from the cross; *life has meaning* because God has lived a human life and died a human death. This is very good news indeed! I believe people can understand redemption if it is explained in such terms because we can relate this to our ordinary experiences. We may not identify our struggles with intimacy as a consequence of the fall, but we experience these struggles anyway. And those who have struggled with intimacy and understand its requisites are sufficiently able to appreciate what God has done through Christ to reconcile the world to himself. The challenge now becomes one of taking up our own crosses to extend this reconciliation to the entire world.

Five

Savior of the World

Perhaps the fallen state of this world can best be illustrated by comparing it with an ideal world. In this ideal world, everything would be oriented toward helping individuals grow in wisdom and in the love of God. Our systems of education, our work, our families, our recreation—everything that belongs to human culture would hold as its focus the true end for which we were created: to know, love and serve God. Consequently, there would be no famine and no wars; there would be health care for the sick; there would be no one lording wealth and power over others; there would be harmony between the human family and all of creation. That we fall so short of the mark of these ideals is proof that we live in a fallen world.

God intended human beings to be partners with him in bringing creation along—to be co-creators. This creation, which is the work of God, is characterized by a global harmony which we are only now beginning to thoroughly appreciate—thanks, in large part, to the research of environmental scientists. Like a great cosmic symphony, all the diverse elements in creation play their unique tunes in perfect obedience to the God within. We, too, once chimed in, contributing our own melodies while harmonizing with the music within and about us. We were God's stewards in creation.

With the fall, we began to play our *own* songs rather than to harmonize with creation. For one thing, we could not even hear the music as in the days of intimacy. Even if we had, however, we were more interested in our own pitiful tunes, and comparing them with one another in jealousy and envy. No longer were different melodies viewed as diverse threads which only enrich the quality of the harmony; differences came to be seen as threats. We became cancerous growths in the mystical body of creation, setting ourselves against creation which is our very source of physical support. And like cancerous cells, we too shall die if we destroy the host which gives us life.

In the language of theology, we would say that original sin becomes ratified in our lives through personal sin—through our personal surrenders to fear and selfishness. The life of the devil thus becomes incarnate in the flesh and, eventually, in the world itself. In our unredeemed efforts to cope with sin, we have chosen pleasure, power, security and status as primary goals for living. Down through the ages, these goals have become deeply entrenched in all our traditions and institutions. Insecurity characterizes the relations among nations and ethnic groups; national boundaries are safeguarded by nuclear arsenals capable of blowing the planet to smithereens; advertising consultants plot ingenious ways to tempt us to spend our money in false pursuits. In short, something like hell has come to this planet; the power of sin has found a stronghold in this world.

Before going much further, it will be helpful to state that in speaking of the sin of the world, we are referring primarily to human culture, and not to natural creation. When we read in the New Testament about being in the world but not of it (Jn 17:14), or about overcoming the world (1 Jn 4:4), we are not being encouraged to despise creation. Indeed, it was precisely *because* we have despised creation that we find ourselves in the predicaments we're in today. Scripture teaches us that creation is good (Gn 1:25). This means that nothing in and of itself can be considered evil. It is when things come under the influence of tainted human nature that they become the instruments of evil. The world, then, refers to those human environmental factors which, as sources of temptation or outright oppression, lead us away from the true end for which we were created. As such, the world is merely an extension of fallen human nature designed to support fallen humanity in its efforts to find meaning in life through pleasure, power, security and status.

Overcoming the World

Of all the writers of the New Testament, no one is so concerned about the world as St. John. In his first epistle, we read:

Have no love for the world,

79

nor the things that the world affords.
If anyone loves the world,
the Father's love has no place in him,
for nothing that the world affords
comes from the Father.
Carnal allurements,
enticements for the eye,
the life of empty show—
all these are from the world.
And the world with its seductions is
     passing away
but the man who does God's will
endures forever (1 Jn 2:15-17).

The world was a force to contend with in the early church, for its allurements constantly called Christians back to that life of sin from which Christ had redeemed them. Not only were there "carnal allurements, enticements of the eye, the life of empty show," but also the threat of execution for those who professed to belong to Christ. What good was freedom from the devil and the flesh, then, if the world only threw it all back in one's face? This was the issue which St. John and the other apostolic leaders had to address. It is yet a burning issue today.

The response of the early church to the power center of sin in the world was Christian community. Christian community became, as it were, a new beginning in the restoration of the old order of creation. If we see the world as a cancerous growth on creation, then we view the church as a new graft of tissue which shall eventually overcome the cancer.

The animating power of the Christian community is the love of God. Through baptism, a Christian comes to enjoy the very life of the Trinity. The Spirit of God becomes an immanent presence in the life of a Christian—a new center for the self. It is this same Spirit which is immanent in all of creation. Thus a Spirit-filled Christian is capable of perceiving again the music of creation and of contributing his or her melodies in the great symphony. Although this harmony between the church and creation became clouded over many times throughout history (largely because of worldly influences in the church), there is evidence from the scriptures that this harmony is considered a natural consequence of the new life in the Spirit. St. Paul alludes to this unity in his letter to the Romans.

> Indeed, the whole created world eagerly awaits the revelation of the sons of God. . . . Yes, we know that all creation groans and is in agony even until now. Not only that, but we ourselves, although we have the Spirit as first fruits, groan inwardly while we await the redemption of our bodies (Rom 8:19, 22-23).

The community of the redeemed recognized its unity with the good-but-disfigured creation, and yearned with creation for its complete restoration.

Just as Christ broke the power hold of the sin in the flesh, so now the Mystical Body of Christ—the church—is commissioned to break the power hold of sin in the world and renew creation. The strategy to be used is none other than the strategy used by Christ to redeem the sin of the flesh: teaching, healing, empathic loving, forgiving and, consequently, transforming. Let us reflect on each of these activities as it manifests itself in the life of the church as an instrument of redemption.

81

Through its ministry of *teaching*, the church points out the meaning of life which is most consistent with our deepest and most authentic nature. We are not accidental products of an indifferent and hostile environment as scientific materialists maintain, but children of God who bear in our souls the image and likeness of our creator. As for the world's enticements to live by pleasure, security and status, the church points out the danger of making these values one's primary meaning in life. So long as one places love first, however, these goals can be kept in balance. As I've written before:

Christianity recognizes the validity of our desires for pleasure, esteem and security and advances a set of propositions about reality which promise to enhance our experiences of each.

1. *Pleasure*: Because Christianity does not espouse a materialistic view of the universe, there is little danger that Christian beliefs can be used to fan the embers of an unhealthy desire for pleasure. More than pleasure, Christianity promises joy, a state of spiritual well-being only hinted at in our experiences of pleasurable sense-gratification (see Jn 15:9-11).

2. *Esteem*: God, the creator and sustainer of the universe, regards each person as precious. To make this experience real, the Holy Spirit moves us to form communities of people committed to affirming the dignity and importance of each individual.

3. *Security*: Even though we all experience accidents and will eventually face death, Christians take heart in their belief in an afterlife.

Because Jesus rose from the dead, we too shall rise to new life. We are immortal spiritual beings, and our heavenly Father's will is ultimately sovereign in the universe. God, our Father, is a providential God, forever leading us into contact with people and circumstances that are grace or help to us in our time of need.

Far from depriving us of the best of human experiences, Christianity enhances them by affirming beliefs which, if we embrace them, allow us to live life to the full (*Becoming a New Person*, Liguori, 1984, pp. 34-35).

A second redemptive activity in the Mystical Body is *healing*. Although faith healing was a common occurrence in the early church and can be noted today, the kind of healing we are talking about here is more related to the healing of loneliness and fear. A community of loving people can go a long way toward healing many of life's emotional hurts. I recall a particularly difficult time in my own life when I was without a job, with my wife in graduate school and small children to care for. The love and support—both material and emotional—which we received from our Christian brothers and sisters was a source of great consolation to us. We did not become discouraged; in fact, we even learned to enjoy ourselves during those hard times.

The relationship between love and healing is a topic which has become of interest to the scientific community. For example, scientists have found that women who are unhappily married have a lower immune response than those who are happily married. Separated and divorced women who grieve the loss of their marriages also have lower immune responses than single women who bear no such grief. When love is lacking, the whole person suffers. It is this healing love which Christian community offers to counteract the destructive darkness of sin in the world.

A third redemptive activity of the church is *empathic loving*. We have heard many times that the church, like Christ, is in the world but not of it (Jn 15:18-19). A common response to this truth has been to withdraw from the world completely in order to avoid contamination. Another response, which is becoming more common among Fundamentalists, is to attempt to create a comprehensive Christian society parallel to the world's (complete with Christian schools, hospitals, auto mechanics, radio and television programs, etc.). The parallel Christian culture response is a well-intentioned effort to provide healthy options for Christians, but it misses the point completely if it presumes to be the means by which the world will be transformed. For one thing, many of these Christian alternatives are not altogether different from their secular counterparts. In addition, there is a kind of snobbery and righteousness in the parallel culture effort which only further alienates hard-core secular folks. Our fallen world will not be transformed by collapsing into a parallel Christian culture, but through the empathy of Christians who live and love *in* the world.

Just as the empathic heart of Christ became vulnerable to the darkness of all of humanity, so must the Mystical Body be open to embracing the darkness of the world. When we withdraw from the world or attempt to create a parallel Christian culture, we are not completely open to being touched by the darkness of the world. In fact, the parallel culture response can set up within us a righteous defensiveness which makes us judgmental—the antithesis of empathic vulnerability. If the Mystical Body does open itself to being touched by darkness, however, there is then the possibility that the light of Christ will shine through this darkness and touch the world with its light. In other words, the world will be converted through love, but we must first love the world *as it is*, just as Christ loved us even when we were sinners.

A church which is open to transforming the world through empathic loving will be free to take a *prophetic stance* when encountering social structures which reinforce the power of sin. The sin of the world is such that we have, through the ages, developed traditions and institutions which serve the power of sin more than love. This is what we mean when we speak of social sin (as opposed to personal sin or original sin). An example would be government policies which condone slavery, or the economic exploitation of certain peoples. These evils must be confronted and opposed just as Christ pointed out some of the excesses of the religious leaders of his day. But it is only a free church—a church which is teaching, healing and loving—which can take such a prophetic stance.

I recall a conversation I had long ago with a bishop about this matter of social sin and prophetic response concerning the activities of a Central American dictator. "We have to be careful we don't upset this leader too much," he said. "If we get this man mad, then he might not allow our priests to say Mass

85

and the people could not fulfill their Sunday obligations." This is but one example of how, many times during our history, we have been a "kept" church, unfree and unwilling to oppose evil because we lost sight of the responsibilities of our call. We often forget that Christians met in the catacombs for almost three centuries, during which time the word "Christian" was synonymous with execution victim. Empathic loving and prophecy are dangerous activities; if we really love in this manner, it could cost us our lives—as it did our Master. A resurrection of new life would follow, however, and this would benefit generations to come.

A final redemptive activity of the church which follows from teaching, healing, empathic loving and prophecy is *forgiving*. We are to love our enemies and pray for our persecutors (Mt 5:43-48). When wronged by others, we must not respond in like manner (Mt 5:38-42). Our response to the evils and injustices of the world must be forgiveness, just as Christ forgave us before we reformed. We hold before the world the possibility of a second chance, a new beginning, if only it will accept our loving invitation to reform and accept its rightful master. Goodness knows the world needs this second chance—and soon! Let us pray that the church may be a loving and forgiving church and so become the harbinger of the kingdom of God that Christ intended for us to be.

Catechetical Implications

The good news here has not so much to do with what Christ has already done, but of what we are now capable of doing because of his victory over sin. Were it not for Christ's victory over the devil and the flesh, we could not hope to transform the darkness of our broken world. The good news is that it is now possible for the reign of God to come on earth as it is in heaven. The catch, however, is that this kingdom must be won by the Mystical Body of Christ through the transforming power of suffering love.

I believe we are just beginning to realize the implications of our baptism. For too long, salvation was viewed as a passive process by Catholics: We had only to receive the sacraments and obey the Ten Commandments and good ship Mother Church would deliver us safely on the shores of eternity. (Many Protestant groups were no better with their smug view of predestination and salvation through faith without works.) In the Catholic church, we also to some extent, seem to have bought into the parallel culture model of transforming the world (although our many schools and hospitals were instituted out of more charitable motives). Since Vatican II, we have largely abandoned this agenda, although we retain many of our old institutions. No longer do we emphasize a passive kind of salvation as in days past.

What is needed today is a widespread recognition that baptism not only initiates us into the community of salvation, but also makes us co-redeemers of the world with Christ. In the beginning, God intended human beings to be co-creators with him in the molding of creation. We bungled that opportunity; but now, through Christ, God has given us a new opportunity to be his partners in the new restoration.

This means that if anyone is in Christ, he is a new creation. The old order has passed away; now all is new! All this has been done by God, who has reconciled us to himself through Christ and has given us the ministry of reconciliation. I mean that God, in Christ, was reconciling the world to himself, not counting men's transgressions against them, and that he has entrusted the message of reconciliation to us. This makes us ambassadors for Christ, God as it were appealing through us. We implore you, in Christ's name: be reconciled to God! (2 Cor 5:17-20).

This notion of being an ambassador for Christ is a powerful idea. Recall that an ambassador is one who represents the interests of a nation or kingdom in a foreign land. The person of the ambassador stands for none other than the ruler of the nation. To abuse an ambassador, then, is to insult the government he or she represents and its leaders; to affirm an ambassador is to make alliance with his or her nation. In other words, as ambassadors for Christ we stand for Christ himself and the kingdom of God. We are his representatives in this world. What we do in behalf of the kingdom is of critical importance; if we don't do this work, it won't get done.

I work with several kinds of Christian share groups, and every now and then I like to ask participants to say who they think they are. The responses I get are fairly predictable: People define themselves in terms of their roles in family, work, hobbies, or dreams for the future. Not once has anyone ever said: "I am an ambassador for Christ!" No one has even said: "I am a minister of the gospel!" Yet that is precisely what we are supposed to be if we are baptized Christians. In the minds of most lay people, however, ministry is still identified with the work of priests, sisters, brothers and other professionals.

The theology of ministry which we so badly need to publicize is already present in the Vatican II documents. The *Decree on the Laity* states quite clearly that the laity

> derive the right and duty with respect to the apostolate from their union with Christ their Head. Incorporated into Christ's Mystical Body through baptism and strengthened by the power of the Holy Spirit through confirmation, they are assigned to the apostolate by the Lord himself. They are consecrated into a royal priesthood and a holy people (cf. 1 Pet. 2:4-10) in order that they may offer spiritual sacrifices through everything they do, and may witness to Christ throughout the world (No. 3).

As cells in the Mystical Body of Christ, each baptized Christian is called to be about the work of that body, which is the transformation of the whole world. We are all called to do our part to combat evil, and we must make it clear that this is a responsibility which belongs to all, not just the "radicals." Baptism calls us to be ambassadors for Christ, and not passive recipients of salvation. This invitation to become co-redeemers has been extended to all. To reject this invitation is to reject Christ himself and his life among us.

We must be careful that this ministry of transformation does not destroy us, however. It is important that those who work for justice be rooted in the Mystical Body, and that they also strive to remain free from the insidious influences of the devil and the flesh. I have known several justice workers who became very self-righteous and angry because of their failure to attend to their own spiritual needs. Some of them became very disillusioned with the church and quit attending services altogether. And indeed, there are many times when church communities do not support those involved in the work of justice, but seem more interested in preserving the status quo. Even so, it is a dangerous business to be about the work of transforming the world without the support of a caring Christian community. A cell cannot live apart from the body for very long. The challenge, then, is often one of first waking up the body so that it can be about its proper business of reconciling the world to God.

A final tiding of good news is that the church is not alone in its work of reconciling. Christ is still with us. With his ascension into heaven, he did not go away—he only disappeared! Seated at the right hand of the Father, he is still true God and true man. Through our relationship with him in faith, we become one with him in the life of the Trinity; but he is also one with us in continuing the work of redemption. We share with him even now in his glory, but he also shares with us in our suffering. Christ continues to carry his cross in the work of his church, and we each must do our own part to "fill up what is lacking in the sufferings of Christ for the sake of his body, the church" (Col 1:24). It is by picking up our own crosses and bearing them in love that we share with Christ in the work of redemption. Paradoxically, this is also the way that leads to the glory of resurrection.

Six

The Way of the Cross

I like to think of my life as an opportunity to become a certain kind of person. Just what kind of person I am to become is pretty much up to me, although the environment in which I grew up has certainly nudged me in specific directions. Nevertheless, the freedom is mine to continue cooperating with those old "tapes," or to begin writing new ones. Because the person I wish to become like is Christ, I see my life as an opportunity to become a new incarnation of God—a conscious, loving, responsive person using my own unique gifts and talents in the service of the kingdom.

Another way of looking at life is to think of it as a school. There are lessons to be learned, and if we learn them well we can pass on to the next grade level. If we fail to learn the lessons implicit in our problems, then we shall have to repeat that class again and again until we get it right. I observe this truth very often during counseling. The divorcee who doesn't learn from her marriage to an abusive alcoholic will marry another abusive alcoholic and go through the torture all over again. It is not until she finally comes to value her own worth that she will begin to seek the company of men who will treat her respectfully. When that happens, she has passed, as it were, from a lower grade to a higher. What scares me many times, however, is the possibility of going through life repeating the same grades again and again. What is the fate of a person who does not learn the lessons he or she was sent here to learn? Perhaps this is where the doctrine of purgatory comes in: We learn it on the other side of death if we have not so totally degenerated as to go to hell.

Tying the ideas of opportunity and schooling together, I see that in order to become a new incarnation of God, there are many lessons I have to learn along the way. Some of these lessons will be difficult for me, but easy for others. Conversely, problems in which others are stuck are sometimes easy for me. Thus the importance of Christian community needs to be underscored. My Christian brothers and sisters, who are also majoring in "Incarnational Realization" can teach and support me in some of my struggles, and I can do the same. We need each other.

There are a few lessons we shall all have to learn because of the effects of sin in our lives. We shall all have to learn that pleasure, power, security, status, esteem and other values are not the true end for which we were created. As fellow students in Incarnational Realization, we can remind each other of this truth, and help each other to submit these worldly values to the higher balancing principles of love of God, neighbor and self. But sometimes simply knowing is not enough. We must also learn from our personal experiences that these values are not capable of delivering the depths of peace and joy for which we all hunger. Only love can bring us to happiness.

Anyone enrolled in Incarnational Realization can expect to encounter conflicts. There is first of all the power of sin in our own flesh, ever persuading us to live by worldly values. Those who have been raised in homes where these values were emphasized will have an especially difficult time growing in love. Then there is the world itself—all those people and institutions and messages which negate the life of love we are striving to live. The devil also works through the flesh and the world and directly in our own minds to negate love and life and happiness. "It's no use," these powers of darkness seem to say. "You can't become an incarnation of God; you're just an old country boy and that's *all* you'll ever be! You don't want to be a Jesus freak anyway, do you? Only the good die young. Christianity is for dullards and moralists—people who don't know how to stand on their own two feet and need a crutch. That's not you. Forget the whole thing; it's a waste of time. Have a beer. Get rich. Look at all those fine-looking women!" And so forth and so on *ad nauseam*. Becoming aware of these voices and the sources which give rise to them is one of the first lessons we must learn in Incarnational Realization.

Jesus tells us:
"Whoever wishes to be my follower must deny
his very self, take up his cross each day, and

JESUS ON THE CROSS—WHY?

follow in my steps. Whoever would save his
life will lose it, and whoever loses his life for
my sake will save it" (Lk 9: 23-24).

There is a self that must be killed (self-one) and a
self that must be gained (self-two). Self-two, the
Christ-self in each of us, cannot emerge unless self-
one—the fearful and selfish ego—is put to death. The
world, the flesh and the devil encourage the cultiva-
tion of self-one; the church encourages the development of self-two. Note, however, the teaching of
Christ that the journey from self-one to self-two is the
way of the cross. Identifying ourselves with Christ requires that we cease identifying ourselves with the
agenda of self-one, and this is a painful struggle. It is
only by accepting this struggle that we make the journey toward a fuller realization of self-two. To shirk the
struggle is to flunk the lesson and consequently to
choose to become a different kind of person—a lesser
incarnation of God.

Here, then, is where it all comes out. With every
decision I make, I write into the law of my being the
kind of person I am becoming. In the last analysis, I
am becoming either a more Christlike person or a
more selfish person. Either way, I will experience conflict and suffering. In the case of self-one, conflict
leads to anger, bitterness and rigidity. But if I accept
my problems and sufferings, I may discover that in
every problem there is a lesson which I have not yet
learned (which is precisely why the problem *is* a
problem). Learning to bear my sufferings and solve
my problems can lead to greater depths of awareness,
empathy and loving responsiveness.

For those enrolled in Incarnational Realization, the cross comes to be recognized as the tool used by God to nurture our growth in those specific areas where we are yet weak. We learn to see our problems not as tormentors (as do students of self-one), but as teachers, and to find in them opportunities to learn new and important lessons about life. The difficult part, however, is to remember all this in the midst of struggles, and to respond to our difficulties in the manner taught by Christ.

Lessons of the Cross

The ultimate challenge for all is to learn to bear our sufferings in such a manner as to continue growing toward the end for which we were created. How, in other words, can we continue to know, love and serve God during our times of trouble? To answer this question, we need only look to Christ, paying careful attention to the manner in which he bore his own sufferings. As he suffered, so must we now suffer. The virtues he has modeled we too must now practice, knowing that the Holy Spirit will be aiding us along the way.

One of the first virtues we notice in Christ is his *acceptance of reality*. He is conscious of the way things ought to be, but this does not prevent him from accepting the people and circumstances of his life just as he finds them. I am reminded here of the story of a man who could not get rid of the weeds in his yard. He tried everything, then finally went to see his minister to help him deal with his frustrations. "If you've tried everything and the weeds still persist, then I suggest you learn to love the weeds," advised the minister. When life deals out sickness or the death of a loved one, we surrender ourselves to these realities while striving to love and grow. Surrendering to reality leads to peace; fighting reality because of some sense of deserving better leads to resentment.

By accepting the realities of our lives, we may come to realize the virtue of *holy indifference*. As St. Ignatius of Loyola explains, "We ought not to be led on by our natural likes and dislikes even in matters such as health or sickness, wealth or poverty, between living in the east or in the west, becoming an accountant or a lawyer." Of course, we do have our own preferences, and we must make decisions about our lives. But the virtue of holy indifference means that we make doing the will of God our highest priority. If we honestly believe that God's will is our happiness, then we strive to choose only that which helps us to do his will—even if it goes against our natural preferences.

A third and related virtue calls for *discernment*. We recognize that there is a time for trying to get rid of weeds, but also a time to surrender to the inevitability of their presence and learn to live with them. There is a time to fight sickness and evil, and a time to surrender oneself into its dark powers. Christ went about teaching and healing for months before finally surrendering himself to the authorities. Several times he escaped their grasp because "his hour had not yet come." Presumably, because he was free, he could have run from this hour and continued in his public ministry, but discernment led him to recognize that the time had come to love in a different way. It is the same with us: We too must learn when it is time to push and time to pull, when to fight and when to surrender. Docility to the Holy Spirit and involvement in a discerning community can help us to recognize the times we are in.

A fourth virtue is *self-control*. In the fighting and/ or surrendering, we must be responsible for our own behavior. Like Christ, we must lay down our life of our own accord and not let others snatch it from us. If pressed to go one mile with another, we surrender to the situation and volunteer to go two; if someone asks for our coats, we give them our shirts as well. Even during those times of pain and turmoil, when it seems that life itself is literally dragging us into the abyss, it is a good thing to voluntarily say, "If I must go into the abyss, then I choose to go of my own accord." This is how we continue to nurture our inner freedom in the face of environmental restrictions. Without this freedom, it is impossible to sustain serenity.

The fifth virtue modeled by Christ is *nonviolent resistance*. We must not make things worse than they already are, nor should we stoop to lower standards of behavior. If someone slaps the right cheek, we offer the left; if they do wrong to us, we make no return in kind. Although we walk in the valley of darkness, we continue to hold to our own standards of behavior, refusing the temptation to give our tormentors a taste of their own medicine. There are practical considerations here as well: Violent resistance will only anger the tormentor—be it a virus or a terrorist, and this is not to our advantage at all. Nevertheless, we would not forget that the word "nonviolent" is only one half of this virtue; "resistance" is called for as well. Although we freely surrender ourselves to accepting our sufferings, it does not follow that we condone or agree with the evils which confront us. Resistance must be offered, but not in such a manner as to increase evil.

The kind of resistance modeled by Christ during his passion is *truthful assertiveness*. Never did he compromise his integrity, nor fail to speak the truth when a hearing was possible. He spoke the truth about himself and his mission to the Sanhedrin, to Pilate, and to the weeping women of Jerusalem on the way to Golgotha. Before Herod he remained silent, however, for Herod had no interest in the truth. The lesson for us is that we, too, should be truthful during times of suffering. In the case of social injustice, we should retain a prophetic stance until the end, like John the Baptist before Herod. During times of sickness, we accept the truth about our situation, then assert ourselves unto wellness in the manner most beneficial toward recovery. Regarding the death of a loved one, we acknowledge our loss and assert our hope for reunion in heaven. "The truth shall set you free," said Christ. During times of struggle, living in the truth and asserting its implications will keep us free.

Forgiveness is the seventh virtue we see modeled by Christ during his passion. The essence of forgiveness is that we hold nothing against those who have hurt us. Resentment is a sign that we have not forgiven, and it is easy to be filled with resentment during times of suffering. It is a property of self-one to resent people, viruses, circumstances, God and even ourselves for the pains that we bear. Forgiveness is the antidote to this kind of poison, which will only deepen our misery. "To forgive is divine," we have heard it said; to forgive is to choose self-two during painful times. But because forgiveness is of the divine, we must pray for the grace to hold nothing

against that which causes us pain. We must also artic-
ulate this forgiveness and make amends if necessary.
By forgiving thus, we become more spiritually free
and, consequently, more capable of making a healthy
response to the causes of our misery. Again we see
that the practicing of spiritual principles yields practical consequences. In the last analysis, all truth is one.

The eighth virtue modeled by Christ is *patient
waiting*. Nothing is forever except God. Of whatever
be the cause of our turmoil, we say "This, too, shall
pass." Christ was able to wait on the Father in this
manner because of another virtue: *trust in providence*.
He knew that God would always provide what was
necessary for one to cope in any given situation, and
that God could draw good out of anything. "We know
that for those who love God, all things conspire to the
good," stated St. Paul (Rom 8:28). By waiting patiently
on the Lord during times of hardship, we open ourselves to the generosity of his providential care for us.
Many times in my own life I have looked back on a
time of hardship and marveled at how it all came out.
In counseling with alcoholics, I have often heard
them say that they are now thankful for their illness
because it led them to Alcoholics Anonymous and a
newer, deeper relationship with God. Through our
times of trials, we learn that the greatest treasure is
not all those worldly things and relationships which
we thought were so important, but the love of the
Lord himself. If we are patient with ourselves and we
pray for the grace to trust in providence, we shall
eventually give praise to God for the good that he
draws out of what appears to the world as loss.

These, then, are nine virtues modeled by Christ
during his passion and death. If we practice these vir-

tues in our own lives, we may continue growing during our times of suffering toward the true end for which we were created. We may learn from our own crosses the lessons we need in order to become new incarnations of God. We also learn a process for transforming the fear and darkness in our own lives.

Conclusions

I suppose it is a truism to state that Christians have troubles just like everybody else. Nevertheless, there are many who still believe that faith leads us into a special kind of relationship with God which absolves us from troubles. It is not uncommon to find Christians, during their times of trouble asking, "How could a good God allow this to happen to me?" The assumption here seems to be that because we are doing something for God—namely, believing in him and striving to live a life of love—then the least God can do for us is to smooth our pathways and oil our squeaky wheels. There is nothing in scripture to support this assumption.

Scripture tells us that we Christians can expect to suffer just like everyone else. In fact, living by faith will probably bring us *more* suffering than if we were to take the path of mediocrity. Christ is very honest with us on this point.

> "Not only will they expel you from
> synagogues;
> a time will come
> when anyone who puts you to death
> will claim to be serving God!" (Jn 16:2).

Christianity goes against the grain of worldly values, and the powers of darkness often respond with violence.

In addition to persecution by the world, Christians sometimes suffer more than others because we are committed to loving. Love leads us to open ourselves to touching and being touched by others. But, as the old saying goes, "When you stretch out your hand in friendship, you sometimes receive a nail." Love brings its own sufferings, a fact which has influenced many to reject loving altogether.

So let us be honest about Christianity and suffering. Dietrich Bonhoeffer rightly concluded that "When Jesus Christ calls a man, he bids him come and die." This is not the kind of slogan that will win many converts, but it is an honest admission that those of us who follow our crucified Master can expect no better than he received.

> "If you find that the world hates you,
> know that it has hated me before you. . . .
> They will harry you
> as they harried me.
> They will respect your words
> as much as they respected mine" (Jn 15:18,20).

If we know these things ahead of time, we won't be surprised when they happen. It might even be a source of consolation to recall, during a time of tribulation, that suffering because one is a Christian is normal. I do not believe we would want it any other way, however. A way of life which does not make risky demands of us is hardly capable of producing greatness of heart.

All of which is not to say that non-Christians do not have their own sufferings. They do, of course. We all suffer natural growing pains, and no one is immune to sickness and accidents. And if it be true that

101

Christian faith and empathic loving bring pain to Christians, then let us acknowledge as well that faithlessness and hard-heartedness bring their own consequences. Which is better: the acute pains and struggles caused by loving, or the numbness, loneliness and mediocrity which follow from avoiding love? These are the choices.

One of the unique contributions of Christianity is its ability to salvage meaning in the face of suffering and death. Because Jesus has suffered and died, we see that God has consecrated all of human life. While the world spends immense measures of psychic energy and money in the effort to avoid what it views as the absurdity of suffering and death, we Christians know that even these experiences have the potential of leading us closer to God. We do not seek suffering for its own sake, of course; the responsibilities of everyday life will bring us trials aplenty. But neither do we fall lock-step into the world's vain efforts to cheat suffering and death. If sufferings come, we attempt to make the best of it; as for death, there is no getting out of it, and the resurrection is a promise that life goes on in new and wonderful ways.

What we learn from Christ, then, is not how to avoid sufferings, but *how to suffer* when we must suffer. It is my opinion that we should teach these lessons on suffering and coping to children from a very early age. The popularity of self-help books which deal with suffering also attest to a hunger among adults for guidance concerning suffering. We all need to learn about stress management practices and basic communication skills so that we can at least begin reducing the intensity of our self-induced pains. A spirituality component would include teachings and suggestions for practicing the nine virtues modeled by Christ which we discussed in the previous section. Finally, it is necessary that a support group component complement our teachings. People need to be able to talk about their struggles, and to hear from others that they are not alone. Many times it is this solidarity which proves to be the key ingredient in helping a person find the courage to bear his or her pains.

As we listen to people share their sufferings, we learn that each person has a different cross to bear at different moments in life. During a recent meeting with a support group which I facilitate, I asked members to complete the statement: "I would be happier if only. . . ." The responses were quite intense. Some wanted more money, some wanted committed lovers, some wanted a better job, and so forth. What was more interesting to me was the open discussion which followed this sharing. Almost every participant would have been willing to trade his or her cross with another's. In fact, a couple of individuals began to minimize the crosses of others, as though they weren't difficult. The individuals who were put down became defensive and began to minimize the problems of their attackers. When I realized what was happening, it was almost too late. We quieted ourselves in a few moments of prayer, then I reminded the group that each person's cross was his or her own, and should therefore be respected and not minimized. If we have already learned the lessons implicit in that cross, then we may perhaps be able to provide helpful guidance and support to the one who still bears it, all the while realizing that this cross is as serious a matter to them as our present crosses are to us. At any rate, self-righteousness is never appropriate when regarding the misery of another. We have only to look to our own struggles to be humbled, for somewhere in this world there is surely a person who would view our own trials as a piece of cake.

The lesson here is that each and every person is always struggling to learn a lesson about life as they progress in Incarnational Realization. This struggle must be respected—even if it seems a small matter to us. Young and old, we're all pilgrims on our way. Those who have learned many lessons may be of use to those who have not, provided that the relationship is characterized by empathy and respect. Never, at any rate, should we do others' homework for them; never should we do for others what they can and ought to do for themselves. Christ gives us a share in his cross that we may come to share in his resurrection; neither must we be overprotective of others. Supportive and helpful we may be when it is appropriate, and when the shoe is on the other foot, we also need to seek the support and counsel of those who have learned many lessons.

We live yet in the age of redemption. The victory over the devil, the flesh and the world won by Christ at Calvary must be consummated by the church, his Mystical Body in space and time. This means that the cells, tissues and organs in that body must become cross-bearers. A church which does not understand the cross and which does little to help its members bear their crosses, will make very little impact in today's world. It is by carrying our crosses together and helping one other become incarnations of God that we most truly become church. Then will the Spirit of God blow fresh among us, joining us with the Father and the Son, who still suffers among his people.

Appendix One
Questions for Reflection and Discussion

Chapter One: Suffering Servant
1. Why was crucifixion considered such a scandalous form of execution during the time of Christ?
2. Why did the Jews want Jesus crucified instead of stoned?
3. How did the prophecies about the suffering servant help the early church to accept the crucifixion of Christ?

Chapter Two: Lamb of God
1. What was the usual function of sacrifices offered to God by the Jews?
2. How did the Lord's supper and the crucifixion fulfill the Passover traditions? What do we mean when we say that Jesus is the Lamb of God?
3. Why did God promise to make a new covenant when there already existed the covenant of Sinai? What are some characteristics of this new covenant?
4. How meaningful to you are these notions of sacrifice and covenant in explaining the meaning of the crucifixion? How meaningful do you think these beliefs are to others?

Chapter Three: Prince of Peace
1. Do you believe in evil spirits? Why? (Why not?)
2. What is the devil's attitude toward human beings? Toward God?

3. How did the crucifixion become Christ's victory march over the powers of Satan?
4. How meaningful to you is the knowledge that Christ has broken the power of Satan? How meaningful do you think this is to others?

Chapter Four: Immanuel
1. Do you believe humanity lives in a fallen state?
2. What consequences do we pay for lack of intimacy with God? Do you experience these consequences in your own life?
3. Explain what we mean when we say that Christ "became sin." How did this help to establish intimacy between God and humanity?
4. How meaningful to you is the "intimacy metaphor" described in this chapter? Do you believe this metaphor is a good way to explain the meaning of the crucifixion to others?

Chapter Five: Savior of the World
1. How has the power of sin become entrenched in the world? Give specific examples and describe how these factors influence your thinking and behavior.
2. What is the proper relationship between humanity and creation? How does sin affect our relationship with creation?
3. How do you feel about being an ambassador for Christ? Do you commonly think of yourself as a co-redeemer?
4. Describe some of the ways in which the church is called to transform the sin of the world. Do you believe the church is faithful in responding to this call? Give examples of ways in which the church is meeting this challenge, and examples of ways in which we are compromising ourselves.

Chapter Six: The Way of the Cross
1. Do you understand your life in terms of an opportunity to become an incarnation of God? Explain your response.
2. What are some of the pains that come from living selfishly? From loving?
3. Why are the nine virtues described in this chapter so important? Which of these virtues challenges you most?
4. What are some of the crosses you are bearing at this time in your life?

Appendix Two
Suggested Reading

New Catechism: Catholic Faith for Adults (New York, NY: Crossroad, 1977). See sections concerning the crucifixion.

Achtemeier, Paul J., Editor: *Harper's Bible Dictionary* (San Francisco, CA: Harper & Row, 1985). See sections on Satan, sacrifice, atonement, crucifixion, covenant, expiation, sin and redemption.

Bishop, Jim: *The Day Christ Died* (New York, NY: Harper & Brothers, 1957).

Brown, Raymond: *Crucified Christ in Holy Week* (Collegeville, MN: Liturgical Press, 1986).

Brown, Raymond, Joseph A. Fitzmeyer and Roland E. Murphy, Editors: *The Jerome Biblical Commentary* (Englewood Cliff, NJ: Prentice-Hall, 1968). See commentaries on passion narratives.

Jones, Alexander, Editor: *The New Jerusalem Bible* (New York, NY: Doubleday, 1985). The footnotes in the passion narratives and in the letters of St. Paul which speak of the crucifixion are most helpful.

Jergens, William A., Ed.: *The Faith of the Early Fathers* (Collegeville, MN: Liturgical Press, 1970). See doctrinal index for writings concerning the incarnation and its purpose.

Lohfink, Gerhard: *The Last Day of Jesus* (Notre Dame, IN: Ave Maria Press, 1984).

McKenzie, John L.: *Dictionary of the Bible* (New York, NY: Macmillan, 1965). See sections on sacrifice, redemption, crucifixion and death.

Kelsey, Morton: *The Cross: Meditations on the Seven Last Words of Christ* (Mahwah, NJ: Paulist, 1983).

Rahner, Karl, S.J., and Herbert Vorgrimler: *Dictionary of Theology* (New York, NY: Crossroad, 1981). See sections on original sin, death, satisfaction theories, redemption and sacrifice.

St. Romain, Philip: *Faith and Doubt Today: Personal Responses to Spiritual Struggles* (Liguori, MO: Liguori Publ., 1986).

St. Romain, Philip: *Jesus Alive in Our Lives* (Notre Dame, IN: Ave Maria Press, 1985).